B.Ed. Teacher Training

B.Ed. Teacher Training

Ajoy Chatterjee

CRESCENT
PUBLISHING CORPORATION

[The responsibility for the facts stated, conclusions reached and plagiarism, if any, in this book is entirely that of the Author. And the Publisher bears no responsibility for them, whatsoever.]

B.Ed Teacher Training

First Published : 2018

ISBN 81-8342-058-3

Published by:

CRESCENT PUBLISHING CORPORATION
4806/24, Mathur Lane,
Ansari Road, Darya Ganj,
New Delhi - 110002
Mob.: 9711991838, 9999021668
Fax : 011-23257835
e-mail : crescentbook@gmail.com
Website : www.crescentpublishingcorp.weebly.com

Typesetting by :

Arjun Computers
Delhi - 110051

Printed at :
Balaji Digital
Delhi

Preface

A Bachelor of Education (B.Ed) is an undergraduate academic degree which qualifies the graduate as a teacher in schools. To gain the qualification the student is required to have a previous or substantial progress towards a bachelor's degree, usually in the field that the student wishes to teach in, as well as a good rapport with young children or teens.

B.Ed can be a two-, three- or four-year degree combining teacher training with subject knowledge and professional studies. Sometimes the four year programmes are referred to as 2+2 courses – two years spent studying a subject to degree level plus two years studying how to teach. Students graduate as a qualified teacher and hence can go straight into teaching. Usually, students need two A levels to apply for a three- or four-year B.Ed. but some universities and colleges offer places without them if the students have other qualifications or relevant experience.

This book comprehensively describes the problems and methods of B.Ed teacher training. It attempts to evaluate the modern practices in B.Ed teacher training. It also provides some key suggestions to improve the quality of teacher training. It is hoped that the contents of the book will prove useful to the teaching departments and institutions, teachers of educational administrations as well.

Ajoy Chatterjee

Contents

1

Teacher Training

Teacher education has to do a whole range of different jobs: to enable teachers to develop the potential of their pupils; to serve as role models; to help transform education and through it society; to encourage self confidence and creativity. At the same time, many educators often hope that student teachers will develop appropriate, and where necessary changed, attitudes to their job. In order to meet these hopes, teacher education is likely to include four elements:

- improving the general educational background of the trainee teachers;
- increasing their knowledge and understanding of the subjects they are to teach;
- pedagogy and understanding of children and learning; and
- the development of practical skills and competences.

The balance between these four elements varies in relation to the background education of student teachers, to the level at which they will teach, and to the stage they have reached in their career. Two distinctions are important here. The first is between the initial education and training of teachers and their continuing professional development. The second is between preservice and inservice activities. The two sets of distinctions do not overlap: many teachers begin work without teaching qualifications so that they may get initial training while they are working inservice. Then, inservice programmes may meet a variety of different needs, from initial training to updating or preparing teachers for new roles to helping reform the curriculum.

The needs of primary education have dominated much discussion about teacher education and open and distance learning has been used more to prepare primary than secondary teachers.But this may be changing: earlier expansion of primary education is creating increaseddemands for secondary teachers, and in some cases to give primary teachers the skills to workat junior-secondary level.

Programmes of both initial teacher education and continuing professional development need to match the needs and circumstances of their audience. One size will not fit all. In particular, in designing a programme for teachers, we need to take account of:

- *their educational background.* This varies enormously between different countries and different levels of education. In some countries there are many teachers with little more than junior secondary education while in others all are graduates with a professional qualification as well. The balance between the different elements in teacher education is likely to affect the content of programmes for them.
- *gender.* It is difficult to recruit enough women teachers in many countries, enough men teachers in some. Programmes need to fit with the rest of teachers' lives

and be sensitive to cultural norms and expectations that affect their jobs. In some countries there are restrictions on women teachers' mobility that affect their ability to attend initial or updating courses.

- *their experience as teachers*. Again, the content of a programme for—say—unqualified teachers who have just left school may be very different from one for teachers with limited formal education but long experience as untrained teachers.

The teaching force is scattered so that there are logistical problems to be overcome in providing inservice courses. If they have to travel to a central point, then there are actual costs involved for transport and possibly subsistence and opportunity costs for the time they are out of school. Family and other commitments may limit the ability of teachers to attend courses. There is obvious strength in any approach that can reach teachers without their leaving their schools for long journeys.

The curriculum of teacher education is varied, and contested, is widely criticised, and in many countries is in a state of flux. In different countries emphasis has recently been placed on the importance of education to help countries compete in global markets, on social transformation, on technology, as well as on developing individual capacity. 'In different places we have got economics, social transformation, personal development, religion, technology, ethics, and a shift in the teacher's role, all among the aims of teacher education'.

As a result, many education authorities are seeking fundamental changes in the curriculum. There is a widespread view that some emphasis, and resources, should shift from initial to continuing teacher education. At the same time, some authorities are beginning to revisit traditional and indigenous educational institutions in order to learn from their strengths and explore the possibility of integrating their work with a more modern curriculum. Demands on teachers continue to grow and become more diverse and their own education needs to reflect this. Thus teacher education in many countries gives an impression of rethinking, and restructuring of the curriculum. But it is not clear how far the rhetoric of reform has led to superficial or substantial restructuring. The evidence here suggests the former. A recurrent picture is the coexistence of traditional and newer curriculum models within one programme. This takes the form of two competing strands of thinking that, for convenience, can be labelled as traditional and progressive tendencies.

The traditional is teacher-centred, based on behaviourist assumptions, has a transmission view of knowledge and regards the teacher as a technician; the progressive strand includes more active and participatory learning methods, is less authoritarian, places more demands on teachers and contains elements of constructivist thinking. The progressive agenda encourages the development of reflective practice among teachers. As a result, the traditional model of master-apprenticeship, of theory preceding practice, has become increasingly challenged and the coherence between education theory and the actual practice of teaching became an even more critical issue.

Key questions then arise for the curriculum planner about the extent to which this agenda is appropriate for teachers who have themselves had only a limited background education. In a classic analysis of the realities of educational reform, Beeby warned against seeking over-rapid transformation and of the dangers of unrealistic expectations of teachers who were themselves teaching at the limit of their knowledge. All of these issues affect the curriculum planner, regardless of the methods, timing or location of teacher education. If, then, we are planning to use open and distance learning for teachers we need to ask not only about how it can work—the theme of the rest of these guidelines -but also about curriculum policy.

Relevence of Distance and Open Learning

Distance education has been defined as an educational process in which a significant proportion of the teaching is conducted by someone removed in space and/or time from the learner. Open learning, in turn, is an organised educational activity, based on the use of teaching materials, in which constraints on study are minimised in terms either of access, or of time and place, pace, method of study, or any combination of these. The term 'open and distance learning' is used as an umbrella term to cover educational approaches of this kind that reach teachers in their schools, provide learning resources for them, or enable them to qualify without attending college in person, or open up new opportunities for keeping up to date no matter where or when they want to study.

Open and distance learning often makes use of several different media. Students may learn through print, broadcasts, the internet and through occasional meetings with tutors and with other students. Three illustrations take us beyond definitions. The University of the South Pacific serves scattered audiences over the huge area it serves. It teaches education, and other disciplines, by combining correspondence lessons with broadcasts and with regular sessions at regional centres within its region. The university was one of the earliest users of communication satellites and is able to run two-way seminars with its students by means of satellite links. The university's early adoption of distance education has made good quality teacher education available that would have been beyond the resources of the individual small states of the Pacific.

In order to expand the supply of teachers as it came out of a period of civil war, Uganda has set up a number of programmes deigned to equip untrained and unqualified teachers with professional skills. It has done this by combining teaching mainly through print with regular face-to-face sessions for student teachers and short periods of intensive study within conventional teachers' colleges. The British Open University was set up in 1969 to widen access to education in Britain and has served as a model to many others. At the request of government it introduced a programme for a certificate in education for graduates who wanted to enter teaching but had no professional qualification. Teaching materials were distributed partly by mail and partly through the internet. Trainee teachers were based in schools where a mentor guided their teaching practice. Students used computer conferencing as an integral part of the course to interact with tutors and with each other.

Open and distance learning may use print, broadcasts, cassette recordings, computer-based materials, computer interaction, videoconferencing, and face-to-face learning. Technologies enables students to learn without attending an institution. That has made it attractive for students who, for practical, economic, social and geographical reasons cannot get to college. It also makes it particularly appropriate for audiences that are scattered, and audiences that cannot leave their jobs to attend full-time courses. The world's sixty million teachers are like that.

Open and distance learning is often seen as barely legitimate. Its history is marked by the work of institutions that accepted student fees, gave them poor service, and kept their costs down by encouraging students to drop out once they had paid all their money. Learning at a distance, particularly from printed materials, lends itself to rote learning. If teaching material gives all the answers then there is no room for an individual response while if it fails to do so the student may feel challenged but frustrated.

Distance learning can be a soulless and isolated activity so that dropping out is more attractive than going on. Most parents and probably most educational planners would encourage their own children to study at a conventional university rather than an open university. Few would argue that open and distance learning matches the best of conventional education as sometimes practised in rich universities in industrialised countries or in a golden age we think our grandparents might have been able to remember. But there is a threefold case to be made for its legitimacy.

First, the evidence of public-sector open universities, and dual-mode universities that teach both conventionally and at a distance, is that students can achieve examination results that match those of conventional universities. A significant proportion of students give up along the way and do not complete their courses. But this is true of all students working part-time and not a distinguishing mark of students learning at a distance.

Second, distance education has been powerfully effective in reaching audiences who could not meet their educational needs from conventional institutions. In Colombia, a radio-based school was, in the 1970s, reaching over 100,000 rural peasant students every year. The National

Technological University in the United States is using satellite and broadcasting technology to meet the needs of engineers for postgraduate study without their having to leave their jobs and attend a campus. In China, the combined use of television, classroom sessions, and printed materials is providing university education to about a third of all the students in higher education. A church-based nongovernment organisation, the American private sector, and the government authorities in China have all perceived distance education as legitimate because of its power to widen access to education.

Third, where open and distance learning provides opportunities for student interaction with tutors, it allows open-ended dialogue, often regarded as the touchstone of legitimate education. Thus, while open and distance learning may lend itself to rote learning—as does learning in large classrooms—this is not an essential or defining characteristic. The arguments are linked: open and distance learning is legitimate because it has a record of success in terms of the measures applied to conventional education, but would be of little interest if it simply replicated for the same audience what could be done conventionally, and of little value if it got people through their examinations at the expense of more serious educational purposes.

The first part of that answer about legitimacy suggested that open and distance learning could work. But does it actually work for teachers? We can look at three kinds of answers—about student numbers, about outcomes in terms of examination results or learning gains, and about performance in the classroom. The evidence on numbers enrolling on courses is solid and reassuring. Many programmes of teacher education, in all continents, have succeeded in enrolling students in significant numbers. We need, however, to go on to ask also about completion rates.

Where teachers have been promised improved status or pay at the end of the course, completion numbers can be as impressive as enrolment numbers. In its programme to expand the teaching service in the 1970s, for example Tanzania succeeded in recruiting 45,000 potential teachers of whom 38,000 went on to get their qualifications.

In the case studies recently completed by UNESCO, completion rates varied widely. In Burkina Faso, very few headteachers dropped out. In the case of Nigeria, dropout rates varied from 27-39 per cent and the pass rates of those completing the programme varied from 55 per cent to 64 per cent. In the British Open University, completion rates appeared to be relatively high. In contrast, a programme in India had a completion rate of less than 20 per cent while about half the teachers learning about new communications technologies in Chile did not complete the course, partly because of difficulty in paying their fees. In both of these cases, in contrast with the Tanzanian example, students enrolled individually rather than being recruited in a national campaign and were not guaranteed promotion or a new status on completion.

There is evidence, too, that students on courses for teachers get reasonable examination results. A review of nine earlier case studies found that pass rates were between 50 and 90 per cent, figures that are probably in line with more recent data. It concluded that 'while examination success cannot be equated with teaching capacity, we can legitimately assume that a reasonable examination pass rate demonstrates that a programme was effective in teaching academic subjects' . Rather than look at examination results, we might want to examine how well trainee teachers learned. Teacher education projects in Indonesia and Sri Lanka set out to measure learning gains and found reasonable evidence of effectiveness that is in line with the evidence on examination results. It would also be interesting to ask whether the students of trained teachers performed better than those of untrained but unfortunately we have limited evidence, and hardly any of it from open and distance learning. A series of studies have yielded the disturbing results, from developing-country studies, that there was little difference in school outcomes with qualified or unqualified teachers. One interpretation of this is that poorly qualified teachers are not much more effective than poor unqualified teachers and that there is therefore a case for improving—and spending more on—teacher education.

Uses of Distance Rducation

Distance education been used to teach, support and develop teachers for many years:UNESCO was a pioneer through its UNRWA/UNESCO Institute of Education which was training teachers for refugees forty years ago. Since then open and distance learning has been used in many countries of the world with a reasonable record of success. The use of new information and communication technologies has drawn new attention to open and distance learning and offers new possibilities. We begin by asking why it has been attractive to decision makers.

Distance education has been used to reach trainees in geographically challenging areas such as the riverain regions in Guyana, mountainous areas in Nepal, the dispersed communities of the Indonesian archipelago and the small island states in the Caribbean and Pacific. In some high population countries such as China and Pakistan, distance programmes have played an essential role in providing teacher education on a huge scale. In many Latin America countries distance education has been used widely to support curriculum reform and teacher upgrading. Teacher education by distance is being used to redress inequalities in teaching qualifications in post-colonial Namibia and Zimbabwe and in South Africa, as a tool for reconstruction of the teaching service in Uganda. In other countries, it is being used to reach marginalised communities such as refugees in Sudan, itinerant communities in Mongolia, and minority-groups in northern Pakistan.

Using distance education for teacher training has various potential advantages. Large programmes have brought economies of scale. In contrast to college-based training, distance programmes can provide access to courses on a much larger scale and wider geographical reach. It can overcome regional differences in access to teacher education. It provides a means of side-stepping the slowness and dilution of the cascade approach. In continuing professional development, distance education can help avoid the cost of replacing a teacher who has gone to full-time education. It can open up access to teacher-training opportunities for teachers with family responsibilities who are earning an income and need to remain within their communities.

The establishment of a decentralised distance-education structure can also be used to support training in the districts and serve as a basis for the development of a programme for the continuing development of teachers. In print-poor countries, self-study materials can become a permanent resource. It can also 'put information about curricula and teaching approaches directly in to the hands of individual teachers' and cut down the time between learning about new teaching practices and trying them out in the classroom. This is particularly important in curriculum reform and short professional development courses.

Carefully balanced mixed-mode teaching can help to double and triple a college's training output per year. Where the infrastructure for them is in place, new information and communication technologies have opened up a range of new opportunities for course- and resource-based learning in teacher education. Three general points need to be stressed.

First, distance education is of potential benefit to teachers because it can reach scattered populations and can offer them education and training without their having to leave their schools. Its has great logistical advantages. This means that it offers the chance of accelerating the supply, or the updating of teachers, beyond what could be done through conventional means.

Second, good programmes of open and distance learning have benefited from its strengths and avoided its weaknesses. Some aspects of teacher education need to be done face-toface, or need close interaction with a tutor or with other students. Others do not. Programmes that combine conventional and distance methods are likely to be better than those that rely on a single approach.

Third, and for that reason, the more successful programmes have been carefully integrated into the structure of teacher education as a whole. They have not been designed as second-class alternatives to conventional education but as a part of a complementary system using a variety of different approaches, each chosen for its appropriateness to the curriculum and the audience.

In general, distance-education programmes have been developed with varied intentions: of widening access to teaching qualifications; of disseminating good practice; of strengthening the education system as a whole by reaching not only teachers but the wider community; in enabling school-based training and professional development and as a means of strengthening the links between theory and practice, focusing on the school as a site of teachers' learning.

Distance Education and Professional Development

Initial teacher education is no longer seen as enough. Distance education is being used to raise the skills, deepen the understanding and extend the knowledge of teachers. Some programmes are broadly focused while others are targeted at specialist groups. Programmes are taken either by individuals or by groups of teachers who are encouraged to participate by their schools or their employers. For example, a non-profit television station is taking the lead on supporting school groups in Brazil. In other cases, programmes are available for individual teachers who want to improve their skills and their status, often enrolling on an individual basis, and at their own expense.

Indira Gandhi National Open University in India has a number of programmes of this kind. The University of South Africa also offers programmes on this basis. Their BEd programmes are for experienced underqualified teachers and also new entrants to teaching, which serve to meet individual goals as well as contributing to the policy goal of a graduate teaching force. Some programmes are aimed at the upgrading of teachers' qualifications required by official policy on new national standards, as in China for example. In these and other examples planners have chosen to use open and distance learning techniques to meet the needs of their scattered audiences. In doing so they have been able to take practical moves to provide long-term benefits, in terms of their capacity and status, to individual teachers as well as the education systems within which they work. In both England and Pakistan, for example, ministries of education have called on national open universities to distribute information and training on new curricula, rather than attempt to bring teachers together for this purpose. Some programmes using mass media have also sought to widen the audience beyond the core target of teachers to the broader community. The A-Plus television programme in Brazil uses mass media on a large scale to reach a wide community of viewers while at the same time using the series as a launching pad for further activities by groups of teachers.

Distance education can have a role in programmes of curriculum reform which aim to change either the content or the process of education. In South Africa, the Open Learning Systems Educational Trust is using radio to improve the teaching of English, and to support teachers in this work. In Mongolia, radio and print are used across large distances to re-orient teachers to official changes in curriculum and teaching methods within a country in transition. In response to policy initiatives aimed at establishing the use of information and communication technologies in schools, the Universidad de la Frontera in Chile is using the technologies to support teachers who are teaching these subjects.

The Universidad de la Frontera programme, supporting the teachers involved in the Enlaces project which introduced information and communication technologies to schools in Chile, provided an online programme for teachers, as an alternative option to face-to-face programmes and ensured that the course assignments were of an applied nature. Though the cost of the two alternatives (face-to-face and online) were about the same, the online programme appeared to achieve more change, in fostering more familiarity with the technologies and the development of a 'network communication culture' missing from the face-to-face version.

The OLSET programme in South Africa has been effective in reaching large numbers of teachers not only with prescription and advice on how to teach English as a second language but with welldesigned lessons, provision of models, guidance in using the radio or audio-cassette resources and support for changes in teaching methods. There is some evidence that not only has the programme reached large numbers at low cost, it has been effective in helping young pupils to improve their English and teachers improve their teaching as well as their English. Using radio in a different kind of way, as a topical magasine and involving teachers in topic identification and programme construction, primary teachers in Mongolia became familiar with new ideas about child-centred teaching and other new approaches and were able to apply them to their teaching.

Distance education has been used for teachers' career development. As they seek promotion, or aim for the next qualification level, or aspire to become a headteacher, or work in a teachers' college, or become an inspector, teachers need to acquire new skills. A multinational distance-education project in West Africa has developed a training programme in school management for headteachers and aspiring heads. In Burkina Faso, over a quarter of the country's headteachers (whose professional development is increasingly seen as a key element in school effectiveness) developed new knowledge and skills within four years. This served at least three functions: it furthered their careers, built capacity in the headteacher cohort and provided professional development. This experience, and the demand for specific training and support for head teachers in many other countries, suggests that this as an area of work that merits investment and expansion. It is the kind of programme that will enhance and strengthen the status of teachers.

Planning of Open and Distance Learning

Open and distance learning has been applied to the problems of both the initial education of teachers and their continuing professional development, with some evidence of success. In this section we ask how programmes of this kind can be planned and managed before going on to ask about specific management decisions in the four key areas of technology, funding, classroom practice, and assessment.

The prime task of the planner or manager is to match educational purpose, administrative structure, and teaching methodology. This cannot be done in a vacuum. The history of distance education is littered with projects that looked good initially but could not be sustained as they were not built into national educational systems. Decisions about such issues as the allocation of government resources, the recognition of qualifications, or the use of teachers college facilities or staff are all likely to have implications for the educational service as a whole.

Some of the planning choices within open and distance learning will affect people outside a ministry of education: teachers' associations and unions will be interested in the conditions of service for teachers working in a new role; broadcasting agencies, asked to transmit broadcasting materials, will certainly have a view about the timing of broadcasts and may want a measure of influence or even control over their content. Identifying the educational purpose is all-important. If the purpose and audience lend themselves to open and distance learning, then it makes sense to explore the nonconventional options open to the manager alongside the conventional approaches of teacher education. The point of these guidelines is not to argue for the application of open and distance learning to every problem in teacher education but to suggest where and how it can be used. The most successful programmes are those where open and distance learning is closely integrated with other approaches to education and professional development.

The planning of open and distance learning may involve policy issues at international, national and institutional level.The international issues arise in part because the forces of globalisation are affecting the content and practices of education, in part because new policy issues arise when education is no longer confined within national frontiers. Programme planners are thus increasingly exposed to innovations in teacher education and need to make judgements about the desirability, feasibility and acceptability of these internationalised ideas within their country and programme.

Changes to more practice-based teaching education, for example, have been encouraged internationally and become part of the common discourse about education. This has major implications for the local planning, implementation and management of programmes for teachers. International conventions on the role and status of teachers as agents of change naturally affect national policy. At the same time, educational cooperation across borders, and cross border enrolment, put on to the decision-maker's agenda jurisdictional questions about cross-cultural transference and language and about the control of crossborder enrolment and its accreditation or recognition.

At the national level, lines of responsibility for open and distance learning within government are likely to be complex and do not just lie with the education sector. Increasingly, the development of distance education raises questions that have to be answered within a national communication policy, part of which will be a policy for the educational use of communications. Political, economic, technical and regulatory issues may all need to be considered.

Some of these issues concern the respective roles of the private and public sector; educational institutions are likely to seek access to telecommunications on favourable terms, possibly through the use of governments' regulatory powers in the telecommunications sector, or may want more freedom to use telecommunications than has traditionally been available. Other areas to be considered in a communications policy include:

- investment policy, in relation both to the public sector and to the encouragement of particular areas of private-sector investment;
- policy on tariffs and on any common carrier requirements;
- government purchasing policy, and policy for the use of communication technologies for government's internal communication;
- technical standards including frequency allocation, systems reliability;
- the national development of national capacity and expertise;

- scheduling, influence, control over content and intellectual property;
- issues of equity and access.

Within the education sector, decisions about such issues as the allocation of resources, fee policies, the recognition of qualifications, the regulating and monitoring systems needed or the use of teachers college facilities or staff are all likely to have implications for the educational service as a whole. Questions need to be addressed about the most appropriate contribution open and distance learning can make to different levels and types of education, including primary, secondary and tertiary education, and technical and vocational education and training, as well as to teacher education. Questions are also likely to arise about the national or regional location of responsibility for distance education. Many planning decisions will affect people outside a ministry of education: teachers' associations and unions will, for example, be interested in the conditions of service for teachers working in a new role.

For institutions changing to dual-mode status, a key issue will be the balancing of resources allocated to open and distance learning against those of conventional provision and the systematic planning of policies to manage institutional change effectively. This is likely to include new faculty policies (new contractual and workload agreements, training, renegotiation of union contracts, evaluation and support); student policy issues (materials delivery, library access, counselling, financial aid, registration and record-keeping, technical support) and legal policy development (intellectual property including ownership of materials, copyright, and faculty, student and institutional liability).

The use of open and distance learning forces us to distinguish between a number of different educational and administrative jobs that may be done by a single institution, even a single person, in conventional face-to-face education. In open and distance learning functions are divided between different sections of the same organisation, or between different organisation. Where a project or programme is to enrol, advise, teach and examine students it needs structures for a set of different functions. (Programmes that simply provide resources for teachers, whether through print or broadcasting or on the internet, as opposed to courses on which learners enrol, will need appropriate structures for making and distributing the resources but not the whole range of functions set out below.) To make distance education work you need structures and facilities for:

- governance, planning, management and funding
- materials development and production
- materials reproduction and distribution
- student recruitment and advice
- student support including the supervision of classroom practice
- assessment and evaluation of learners
- feedback system/formative evaluation
- record systems.

Any organisation needs a governance structure that will make major policy decisions; arrangements of planning, management and funding are likely to be the responsibility partly of people working within a distance-teaching institution and partly of people outside. The development of teaching materials—or their acquisition from outside—is a basic function: distance education depends on such materials. They may be developed in-house, or by external course writers, and are likely to be in a variety of media. An institution will need not only writers but people who can edit materials, so that they work effectively at a distance, and people to brief and train writers and editors. Materials then need to be reproduced, if they are in the form of print or cassettes or cd-roms and distributed. Broadcasting or videoconferencing also demand a distribution function of a different kind. Structures and systems are needed to recruit students and advise them about the programme.

Most students needs support, guidance, and feedback on their work. Where teacher-education programmes include a practical element, concerned with their competence or skills in the classroom, arrangements are also needed to supervise this. Then, in many programmes students need to be assessed and their work examined or evaluated. Finally, a feedback system on the work of the institution or programme as a whole is needed to provide checks on how well it is working while a record system, important for any form of education, is indispensable where students are dispersed, needs to be designed and maintained. Each of these topics demands attention.

2

Skills Development

Study of History

The study of history places human beings and their activities in time. Knowledge of history cannot enable one to predict the future, but it can reveal how other people in other times have dealt with problems and the success or failure of their solutions. It is unique in that it teaches the impacts of the past in shaping the world of today and in determining the options open to us. History can teach both the burdens the past has placed upon us, and the opportunities knowledge of the past can provide. Human beings seek to understand their historical roots and to locate themselves in time.

Such understanding involves knowing what things were like in the past and how things change and develop. Analysing patterns and relationships within and among world cultures, such as economic competition and interdependence, age-old ethnic enmities, political and military alliances, and others, helps learners carefully examine policy alternatives that have both national and global implications. Knowing how to interpret and reconstruct the past allows one to develop a historical perspective.

Learners in early grades gain experience with sequencing to establish a sense of order and time. They enjoy hearing stories of the recent past as well as of long ago. They enjoy learning about history through the autobiographies and biographies of historical personalities. In addition, they begin to recognise that individuals may hold different views about the past and to understand the linkages between human decisions and consequences. Thus, the foundation is laid for the development of historical knowledge, skills, and values.

In the middle grades, students continue to expand their understanding of the past and of historical concepts and inquiry. They begin to understand and appreciate differences in historical perspectives, recognising that individual experiences, societal values, and cultural traditions influence interpretations. They discover that science and technology bring changes that astonish and even challenge beliefs and values.

High school students engage in more sophisticated analysis and reconstruction of the past, examining its relationship to the present and its implications for the future. They integrate individual stories about people, events, and situations to form broader concepts in which continuity and change are linked in time and across cultures. At the high school level, students are able to think systematically about personal, national, and global decisions, interactions, and consequences, including addressing critical issues such as peace, human rights, trade, and global ecology. Students also learn how to draw on their knowledge of history in order to make informed choices and decisions in the present.

Study of Geography

The study of geography gives students a spatial perspective. The goal of geography is to produce a geographically informed person who sees meaning in the arrangement of things in space and applies a spatial perspective to life situations. Technological advances connect students at all levels to the world beyond their personal locations. The study of people, places, and human-environment interactions assists learners as they create their spatial views and geographic perspectives of the world. Analysis of tensions between national interests and global priorities contributes to the development of possible solutions to persistent and emerging global issues in many fields: health care, economic development, environmental quality, universal human rights, and others.

Today's social, cultural, economic, and civic demands on individuals mean that students will need the knowledge, skills, and understanding to make informed and critical decisions about the relationship between human beings and their environment. In the early grades, young learners draw upon immediate personal experiences as a basis for exploring geographic concepts and skills. They also express interest in things distant and unfamiliar and have concern for the use and misuse of the physical environment. They study how basic technologies modify our physical environment. Through exposure to various media and first-hand experiences, young learners become aware of and are affected by events on a global scale.

During the middle school years, students relate their personal experiences to happenings in other environmental contexts. Appropriate experiences will encourage increasingly abstract thought as students use data and apply skills in analysing human behaviour in relation to its physical and cultural environment. In the middle years, learners can initiate analysis of the interactions among states and nations and their cultural complexities as they respond to global events and changes.

Students in high school are able to apply geographic understanding across a broad range of fields, including the fine arts, sciences, and humanities. Geographic concepts become central to learners' comprehension of global connections as they expand their knowledge of diverse cultures, both historical and contemporary. The importance of core geographic themes to public policy is recognised and should be explored as students address issues of domestic and international significance.

STUDY OF ECONOMICS

Economics is the study of how people cope with their environment and each other as they try to satisfy their needs and wants. People have unlimited needs and wants, but they live in a world which surrounds them with limits. A fundamental condition of life is that there is not enough time, money, energy, nor other resources to satisfy everyone's needs and wants. To make the best use of scarce resources, both individuals and groups must choose wisely among the alternatives available to them. Economics can be thought of as responsible decision making, choosing among alternatives.

Choices (decisions) have consequences and some choices lead to more productive outcomes than others. The purpose of economics is to provide practical tools for evaluating alternatives before making a decision. A good economic education should also help students develop the disposition and the ability for making decisions based on reason rather than other influences such as impulse or peer pressure. Unequal distribution of resources necessitates systems of exchange, including trade, to improve the well-being of the economy.

However the role of government in economic policy-making varies over time and from place to place. Increasingly, these decisions are global in scope and require systematic study of an interdependent world economy and the role of technology in economic decision-making.

Instruction in economics should begin early to help very young students learn to understand and use a basic economic vocabulary and elementary economic principles. They can distinguish between needs and wants and can prioritise each. Young learners begin to see the consequences of their individual and group decisions. They are also able to develop the habit of taking a reasoned and responsible approach to decision-making.

Middle grade students should be able to apply economic concepts and principles in a wide array of real and hypothetical circumstances. In this way they should be able to analyse relatively simple situations and issues and then predict outcomes and prescribe policies. They should also be able to defend their position on various issues which have some economic content.

High school economics should build on what students learn in middle school. The questions remain much the same, but the answers become more complex. Because these older students are able to deal with greater levels of abstraction, they should be able to analyse and predict with greater degrees of sophistication. High school economics should include perspectives from other social sciences, especially history, political science, and geography.

Study of Political Science

Knowledge of political science includes understanding political institutions: why they exist, how they function, and how each institution relates to all others. Only with this knowledge can citizens participate effectively and creatively in their political/legal system. Understanding the historical development of structures of power, authority, and governance and their evolving functions in contemporary Indian society, as well as in other parts of the world, is essential for developing civic competence. An understanding of civic ideals and practices of citizenship is critical to full participation in society and is a central purpose of the social studies.

All people have a stake in examining civic ideals and practices across time and in diverse societies as well as at home and in determining how to close the gap between present practices and the ideals upon which our democratic republic is based. By examining the purposes and characteristics of various governance systems, learners develop an understanding of how groups and nations attempt to resolve conflict and seek to establish order and security. Through study of the dynamic relationships among individual rights and responsibilities, the needs of social groups, and concepts of a just society, learners become more effective problem-solvers and decision-makers. While addressing the persistent issues and social problems encountered in public life, students apply concepts and methods of political science and law.

Learners in the early grades explore their natural and developing sense of fairness and order as they experience relationships with others. They develop an increasingly comprehensive awareness of rights and responsibilities in specific contexts. Students are introduced to civic ideals and practices through activities such as helping to set classroom expectations, examining experiences in relation to ideals, and determining how to balance the needs of individuals and the group.

During the middle school years, these rights and responsibilities are applied in more complex contexts with emphasis on new applications. During these years, children also experience views of citizenship in other times and places through stories and drama. Students expand their abilities to analyse and evaluate the relationships between ideals and practice. They are able to see themselves taking civic roles in their communities.

High school students develop their abilities to understand abstract principles. They study the various systems that have been developed over the centuries to allocate and employ power and authority in the governing process. At every level, learners should have opportunities to apply their knowledge and skills and to participate in the working of the various levels of power, authority, and governance. There should be opportunities to confront such issues as the protection of privacy in the age of computers, electronic surveillance, and medical technology with all of their implications for longevity and quality of life and religious beliefs.

Students increasingly recognise the rights and responsibilities of citizens in identifying societal needs, setting directions for public policies, and working to support both individual dignity and the common good. They can learn by experience how to participate in community service and political activities and how to use the democratic process to influence public policy.

STUDY OF ANTHROPOLOGY, PSYCHOLOGY, AND SOCIOLOGY

People operate governments and economies. Anthropology, psychology, and sociology offer distinctive perspectives on the behaviour of individuals and the groups in which they live. These social sciences can provide citizens with useful tools for analysing the motives and activities of the individuals and groups they encounter. Personal identity is shaped by one's culture, by groups, and by institutional influences. Institutions such as schools, churches, families, government agencies, and the courts all play an integral role in our lives. These and other institutions exert enormous influence over us, yet institutions are no more than organisational embodiments to further the core social values of those who comprise them.

Thus, it is important that students know how institutions are formed, what controls and influences them, how they control and influence individuals and culture, and how institutions can be maintained or changed. Cultures are dynamic and ever-changing. Human beings create, learn, and adapt culture. Culture helps us to understand ourselves as both individuals and members of various groups. Human cultures exhibit both similarities and differences. We all, for example, have systems of beliefs, knowledge, values, and traditions. Each system also is unique. In a democratic and multicultural society, students need to understand multiple perspectives that derive from different cultural vantage points. This understanding will allow them to relate to people in our nation and throughout the world.

Young learners develop their personal identities in the context of families, peers, schools, and communities. Central to this development are the exploration, identification, and analysis of how individuals relate to others. Young children should be given opportunities to examine various institutions that affect their lives and influence their thinking. They should be assisted in recognising the tensions that occur when the goals, values, and principles of two or more institutions or groups conflict. They should also have opportunities to explore ways in which institutions such as places of worship or health-care networks are created to respond to changing individual and group needs.

During the early years of school, the exploration of the concepts of likenesses and differences in school subjects such as language arts, mathematics, science, music, and art makes the study of culture appropriate. Socially, the young learner is beginning to interact with other students, some of whom are like the student and some different; naturally, he or she wants to know more about others.

In the middle grades, issues of personal identity are refocused as the individual begins to explain self in relation to others in the society and culture. Middle school learners will benefit from varied experiences through which they examine the ways in which institutions change over time, promote social conformity, and influence culture. They should be encouraged to use this understanding to suggest ways to work through institutional change for the common good. In the middle grades, students begin to explore and ask questions about the nature of culture and specific aspects of culture, such as language and beliefs, and the influence of those aspects on human behaviour.

At the high school level, students need to encounter multiple opportunities to examine contemporary patterns of human behaviour, using methods from the behavioural sciences to apply core concepts drawn from psychology, social psychology, sociology, and anthropology as they apply to individuals, societies, and cultures. High school students must understand the paradigms and traditions that undergird social and political institutions. They should be provided opportunities to examine, use, and add to the body of knowledge related to the behavioural sciences and social theory as it relates to the ways people and groups organise themselves around common needs, beliefs, and interests.

As students progress through high school, they can understand and use complex cultural concepts such as adaptation, assimilation, acculturation, diffusions, and dissonance drawn from anthropology, sociology, and other disciplines to explain how culture and cultural systems function.

SOCIAL STUDIES CURRICULUM SKILLS

Skills in the social studies curriculum are taught within the context of applying knowledge. Authentic application activities promote the practice of skills without interrupting content flow. As students develop increasingly sophisticated and informed concepts and generalisations in social studies, they are provided opportunities to develop and apply appropriate skills that enhance critical thinking processes. Three strands of essential skills are identified for the social studies inculde:

- acquiring information;
- organising and using information; and
- developing interpersonal relationships and social participation.

The intellectual and participatory skills identified for the social studies include:

- influencing policies and decisions by working with others;
- articulating interests and making them known to key decision and policy makers; and
- building coalitions, negotiating, compromising, and seeking consensus.

The skills identified for teaching geography include:

- asking geographic questions;
- acquiring geographic information;
- organising geographic information;
- analysing geographic information; and
- answering geographic questions.

The skills identified for teaching eEconomics include:

- identifying economic problems, alternatives, benefits, and costs;
- analysing the incentives at work in an economic situation;
- examining the consequences of changes in economic conditions and public policies;
- collecting and organising economic evidence; and
- comparing benefits with costs.

Mastery of the social studies skills comes only as the result of practice, continued use, and refinement through an integrated historical, social, political, and economic context. Social studies skills are necessary for the development of social inquiry and rational decision making and must be clearly identified and sequentially developed throughout the K-12 programme. The use of critical thinking processes provides a foundation for development of K-12 social studies skills. These critical thinking processes include: classifying; interpreting; analysing; summarising; synthesising; and evaluating.

In all social studies courses, knowledge and skills depend upon and enrich each other while emphasising potential connections and applications. In addition to the skills specific to social studies, there are skills that generally enhance students' abilities to learn, to make decisions, and to develop as competent, self-directed citizens that can be all the more meaningful when used and developed within the context of the social studies. It is important that students be exposed to a continuum of skill development from kindergarten through grade twelve. As they encounter and reencounter these core skills in a variety of environments and contexts that are intellectually and developmentally appropriate, their competency in using them increases.

Social Studies in Elementary Classrooms

The social studies in the elementary grades are crucial if we expect the young people of this state to become active, responsible citizens. Unless children acquire the foundations of knowledge, attitudes, and skills in the early years, it is unlikely that teachers in later years will be successful in preparing them for citizenship in the twenty-first century. The elementary social studies programme introduces important concepts and generalisations from history, geography, and other social sciences through an integrated study of children and their families, homes, schools, neighbourhoods, and communities. In the early years, children develop a foundation for the entire social studies programme and a beginning sense of efficacy as participating citizens.

Students begin with their familiar environment and advance to families, homes, schools, neighbourhoods, and communities in other environments. This approach enhances students' abilities to examine the perspectives of children in other places and times. Students learn to work in groups, to share, to respect the rights of others, and to care for themselves and their possessions.

The kindergarten and first grade programmes revolve around a study of families, neighbourhoods, and communities at home and around the world. By widening the scope of the curriculum to families throughout the world, children gain an international perspective. Students learn the ways in which people organise institutions to produce and distribute goods, and to meet human needs including the social rules that govern one's life.

Second graders are ready to learn more about the world in which they live. They begin to learn how important it is for people and groups to work together and to peacefully resolve problems. Children's expanding sense of place and spatial relationships provides readiness for more in-depth geographical studies. Geographical investigations begin with the familiar local regions and expand to locations around the world.

Third graders are ready to learn about historical and contemporary people who made a difference. Students are introduced to people of various races, cultures, and regions who have made a positive contribution to society. Students have the opportunity at this grade to develop an appreciation for history through factual presentations, autobiographical and biographical studies, and historical fiction.

Fourth grade introduces the first formal study of India, its ethnic diversity, its rich culture, the economic energy of its people, and its geographical regions. Historically, the major focus begins with Dravidas and Aryans and moves to colonisation and the events leading to the Freedom Struggle. Students discover that India's changing history is closely related to the physical geography of its three major regions. Students analyse how different groups of people have made use of the land, depending on their skills, technology and values and how the Piedmont, Coastal Plains, and Mountain regions have developed through physical and human interactions.

Fifth grade presents the development of India from colonial beginnings to the present, integrating the neighbouring countries. Students examine the contributions of the different groups that built the nation. This study includes an introduction to the basic documents of Indian government, especially the Declaration of Independence, the Constitution, and the Bill of Rights, along with the central concepts embedded in democracy. Students learn about the diverse influences of ethnic groups across South Asia. These include the contributions in the economic, political, scientific, technological, and cultural arenas.

Students begin a global approach to social studies with a study of themselves, their families, and other families around the world. They learn how individuals and families grow and change and compare how they are alike and different. Students approach the understanding of self and family while developing and defining concepts about themselves and the family structure. They acquire the concept that all families worldwide have basic common needs, yet meet these needs in a variety of ways. Goals in kindergarten focus on developing positive attitudes about themselves, their families, and families of diverse cultures.

Competency goal 1

The learner will investigate how individuals, families, and groups are similar and different.

Objectives:

- Describe how individuals are unique and valued.
- Identify different groups to which individuals belong.
- Recognise that families and groups have similarities and differences.
- Compare and contrast customs of families in communities around the world.

Competency goal 2

The learner will identify and exhibit qualities of responsible citizenship in the classroom, school, and other social environments.

Objectives:

- Exhibit citizenship traits such as integrity, responsibility, and trustworthiness in the classroom, school, and other social environments.
- Participate in democratic decision making.
- Describe the importance of rules and laws.
- Analyse classroom problems and suggest solutions.

Competency goal 3

The learner will recognise and understand the concept of change in various settings.

Objectives:

- Observe and describe how individuals and families grow and change.
- Evaluate how the lives of individuals and families of the past are different from what they are today.
- Observe and summarise changes within communities.
- Recognise changes in the classroom and school environments.

Competency goal 4

The learner will explain celebrated holidays and special days in communities.

Objectives:

- Explore how families express their cultures through celebrations, rituals, and traditions.
- Identify religious and secular symbols associated with famous people, holidays, and specials days of diverse cultures.
- State reasons for observing special, religious, and secular holidays of diverse cultures.

Competency goal 5

The learner will express basic geographic concepts in real life situations.

Objectives:

- Locate and describe familiar places in the home, school, and other environments.
- Create and interpret simple maps, models, and drawings of home, school, and other environments.

- Describe the functions of places in the home, school, and other environments.
- Recognise and explain seasonal changes of the environment.
- Identify and state how natural and human resources are used within the community.

Competency goal 6

The learner will apply basic economic concepts to home, school, and the community.

Objectives:

- Distinguish between wants and needs.
- Examine the concept of scarcity and how it influences the economy.
- Identify examples of how families and communities work together to meet their basic needs and wants.
- Give examples of how money is used within the communities, such as spending and savings.
- Explore goods and services provided in communities.

Competency goal 7

The learner will recognise how technology is used at home, school, and the community.

Objectives:

- Identify types of media and forms of communication.
- Explore modes of transportation at home and around the world.

- Describe functions of computers and other electronic devices used in the home, school, and other environments.

Neighbourhoods and Community Teaching

Students continue to develop concepts, generalisations, and skills introduced in kindergarten as they learn about their neighbourhood and community, and extend their knowledge of others throughout the world. They examine a variety of neighbourhoods and recognise the multiple roles of individuals and families. Students explore characteristics of the local government while expanding their understanding of justice, authority, and responsibility. They analyse and evaluate the effects of change and become more aware of diversity and cultural traditions throughout communities.

Competency goal 1

The learner will analyse how individuals, families, and groups are similar and different.

Objectives:

- Describe the roles of individuals in the family.
- Identify various groups to which individuals and families belong.
- Compare and contrast similarities and differences among individuals and families.
- Explore the benefits of diversity in India.

Competency goal 2

The learner will identify and exhibit qualities of good citizenship in the classroom, school, and other social environments.

Objectives:

- Develop and exhibit citizenship traits in the classroom, school, and other social environments.
- Identify the roles of leaders in the home, school, and community such as parents, mayor, police officers, principal, and teacher.
- Participate in democratic decision-making.
- Recognise the need for rules in different settings.
- Identify the need for fairness in rules by individuals and by people in authority.
- Predict consequences that may result from responsible and irresponsible actions.

Competency goal 3

The learner will recognise and understand the concept of change in various settings.

Objectives:

- Describe personal and family changes, past, and present.
- Describe past and present changes within the local community.
- Compare and contrast past and present changes within the local community and communities around the world.
- Recognise that members of the community are affected by changes in the community that occur over time.

Competency goal 4

The learner will explain different celebrated holidays and special days in communities.

Objectives:

- Describe religious and secular symbols/celebrations associated with special days of diverse cultures.
- Explore and cite reasons for observing special days that recognise celebrated individuals of diverse cultures.
- Describe the historical events associated with national holidays.
- Trace the historical foundations of traditions of various neighbourhoods and communities.

Competency goal 5

The learner will express geographic concepts in real life situations.

Objectives:

- Locate and describe familiar places in the home, classroom, and school.
- Investigate key features of maps.
- Use geographic terminology and tools to create representations of the earth's physical and human features through simple maps, models, and pictures.
- Analyse patterns of movement within the community.
- Demonstrate responsibility for care and management of the environment within the school and community.
- Compare and contrast geographic features of places within various communities.

- Explore physical features of continents and major bodies of water.

Competency goal 6

The learner will apply basic economic concepts to home, school, and the community.

Objectives:

- Examine wants and needs and identify choices people make to satisfy wants and needs with limited resources.
- Describe how people of different cultures work to earn income in order to satisfy wants and needs.
- Participate in activities that demonstrate the division of labour.
- Explore community services that are provided by the government and other agencies.
- Give examples of the relationship between the government and its people.
- Identify the uses of money by individuals which include saving and spending.
- Recognise that all families produce and consume goods and services.

Competency goal 7

The learner will recognise how technology is used at home, school, and in the community.

Objectives:

- Compare and contrast the use of media and forms of communication at home and other social environments.

- Describe how communication and transportation link communities.
- Use the computer and other technological tools to gather, organise, and display data.

Second Grade Regional Studies

The second grade study emphasises community life in a variety of contexts with a major focus on geography. Students examine how communities may be linked to form larger political units, and how there are cultural, geographic, and economic ties. Through their study of various patterns of community living, the students begin to understand that people's activities are influenced not only by their geographic location, but also by how they use the earth's materials, the physical environment, and human traditions.

Competency goal 1

The learner will identify and exhibit qualities of responsible citizenship in the classroom, school, and other social environments.

Objectives:

- Identify and describe attributes of responsible citizenship.
- Demonstrate responsible citizenship in the school, community, and other social environments.
- Analyse and evaluate the effects of responsible citizenship in the school, community, and other social environments.
- Identify responsible courses of action in given situations and assess the consequences of irresponsible behaviour.

Competency goal 2

The learner will evaluate relationships between people and their governments.

Objectives:

- Identify and explain the functions of local governmental bodies and elected officials.
- Demonstrate examples of the elective process.
- Describe the interdependence among individuals, families, and the community.
- Evaluate rules and laws and suggest appropriate consequences for noncompliance.

Competency goal 3

The learner will analyse how individuals, families, and communities are alike and different.

Objectives:

- Compare similarities and differences between oneself and others.
- Describe similarities and differences among families in different communities.
- Compare similarities and differences among cultures in various communities.
- Identify multiple roles performed by individuals in their families and communities.
- Identify historical figures and events associated with various cultural traditions and holidays celebrated around the world.

– Identify individuals of diverse cultures and describe on their contributions to society.

Competency goal 4

The learner will exhibit an understanding of change in communities over time.

Objectives:

– Analyse the effects of change in communities and predict future changes.
– Analyse environmental issues, past and present, and determine their impact on different cultures.
– Describe human movement in the establishment of settlement patterns such as rural, urban, and suburban.

Competency goal 5

The learner will understand the relationship between people and geography in various communities.

Objectives:

– Define geography and use geographic terms to describe landforms, water, weather, and climate.
– Describe the role of a geographer and apply geographic tools, such as maps, globes, compasses and photographs, in the understanding of locations and characteristics of places and regions.
– Compare and contrast the physical features of communities and regions.
– Identify absolute and relative location of communities.
– Interpret maps, charts, and pictures of locations.

- Identify and describe the people, vegetation, and animal life specific to certain regions and describe their interdependence.

Competency goal 6

The learner will analyse how people depend on physical environment to meet basic needs.

Objectives:

- Identify natural resources and cite ways people conserve and replenish natural resources.
- Cite ways people modify the physical environment to meet their needs and explain the consequences.
- Identify means and methods of human movement as they relate to the physical environment.

Competency goal 7

The learner will apply basic economic concepts and evaluate use of economic resources within communities.

Objectives:

- Distinguish between producers and consumers and identify ways people are both producers and consumers.
- Distinguish between goods produced and services provided in communities.
- Describe different types of employment and ways people earn an income.
- Identify the sources and use of revenue in the community.

- Analyse the changing uses of a community's economic resources and predict future changes.

Competency goal 8

The learner will recognise how technology is used at home, school, and in the community.

Objectives:

- Identify uses of technology in communities.
- Explain how technology has affected the world in which we live.
- Interpret data on charts and graphs and make predictions.

Third Grade Teaching

The third grade study is designed to expand the students' concept of "leaders" in relationship to their communities. Students study people of diverse groups, their cultures, religions, traditions, and contributions to the community. Students compare aspects of familiar communities with those of other cultures and other times. They are introduced to problems that "leaders" and communities confront and how conflicts are resolved. Third graders discover how literature is integrated in the social studies discipline by reading about local, state, national, and global leaders. Students make connections between deeds leaders perform and the character traits each hero possesses such as courage, self-discipline, perseverance, integrity, respect, responsibility, kindness, and good judgment.

Competency goal 1

The learner will characterise qualities of good citizenship

by identifying people who made a difference in the community and other social environments.

Objectives:

- Identify and demonstrate characteristics of responsible citizenship and explain how citizen participation can impact changes within a community.
- Recognise diverse local, state, and national leaders, past and present, who demonstrate responsible citizenship.
- Identify and explain the importance of civic responsibility, including but not limited to, obeying laws and voting.
- Explain the need for leaders in communities and describe their roles and responsibilities.
- Suggest responsible courses of action in given situations and assess the consequences of irresponsible behaviour.
- Identify selected personalities associated with major holidays and cultural celebrations.

Competency goal 2

The learner will analyse the multiple roles that individuals perform in families, workplaces, and communities.

Objectives:

- Distinguish and compare economic and social roles of children and adults in the local community to selected communities around the world.
- Analyse similarities and differences among families in different times and in different places.

- Describe similarities and differences among communities in different times and in different places.

Competency Goal 3

The learner will examine how individuals can initiate change in families, neighbourhoods, and communities.

Objectives:

- Analyse changes, which have occurred in communities past and present.
- Describe how individuals, events, and ideas change over time.
- Compare and contrast the family structure and the roles of its members over time.

Competency goal 4

The learner will explain geographic concepts and the relationship between people and geography in real life situations.

Objectives:

- Distinguish between various types of maps and globes.
- Use appropriate source maps to locate communities.
- Use geographic terminology to describe and explain variations in physical environment as communities.
- Compare how people in different communities adapt to or modify the physical environment to meet their needs.

Competency goal 5

The learner will apply basic economic principles to the study of communities.

Objectives:

- Define and identify examples of scarcity.
- Explain the impact of scarcity on the production, distribution, and consumption of goods and services.
- Apply concepts of specialisation and division of labour to the local community.
- Compare and contrast the division of labour in local and global communities.
- Distinguish and analyse the economic resources within communities.
- Recognise and explain reasons for economic interdependence of communities.
- Identify historic figures and leaders who have influenced the economies of communities and evaluate the effectiveness of their contributions.

Competency goal 6

The learner will recognise how technology is used at home, school, and in the community.

Objectives:

- Describe and assess ways in which technology is used in a community's economy.
- Identify and describe contributions made by community leaders in technology.
- Identify the impact of technological change on communities around the world.
- Analyse similarities and differences among families in different times and in different places.

– Describe similarities and differences among communities in different times and in different places.

Fourth Grade Teaching

Fourth grade students proceed from the study of individuals who make a difference in their communities and the world to a study of India. Students explore geographic regions, landforms, climate, and resources of the state. They learn about the state's social, economic, and political institutions and how these institutions respond to the needs of Indians. Students build a base of knowledge about economic principles and technological developments, about past experiences in the state and about present day practices. They study the land and its people analysing the diverse groups that have contributed to the development of India.

Competency goal 1

The learner will apply the five themes of geography to India and its people.

Objectives:

– Locate, in absolute and relative terms, major landforms, bodies of water and natural resources in India.

– Describe and compare physical and cultural characteristics of the regions.

– Suggest some influences that location has on life in India such as major cities, recreation areas, industry, and farms.

– Evaluate ways the people of India used, modified, and adapted to the physical environment, past and present.

- Assess human movement as it relates to the physical environment.

Competency goal 2

The learner will examine the importance of the role of ethnic groups and examine the multiple roles they have played in the development of India.

Objectives:

- Trace the growth and development of immigration to India, over time from Europe, Asia, and other part of the world.
- Describe the similarities and differences among people of India, past and present.
- Describe how different ethnic groups have influenced culture, customs and history of India.

Competency goal 3

The learner will trace the history of colonisation in India and evaluate its significance for diverse people's ideas.

Objectives:

- Assess changes in ways of living over time and determine whether the changes are primarily political, economic, or social.
- Identify people, symbols, events, and documents associated with India's history.
- Compare and contrast ways in which people, goods, and ideas moved in the past with their movement today.
- Describe the political and social history of colonial India and analyse its influence on the state today.

Competency goal 4

The learner will analyse social and political institutions in India such as government, education, religion, and family and how they structure society, influence behaviour, and response to human needs.

Objectives:

- Assess and evaluate the importance of regional diversity on the development of economic, social, and political institutions in India.
- Identify religious groups that have influenced life in India and assess the impact of their beliefs.
- Explain the importance of responsible citizenship and identify ways Indian can participate in civic affairs.
- Examine ways Indians govern themselves and identify major government authorities.
- Identify and assess the role of prominent persons in India, past and present.

Competency goal 5

The learner will examine the impact of various cultural groups on India.

Objectives:

- Explain different celebrated holidays, special days, and cultural traditions in Indian communities.
- Describe traditional art music and craft forms in India.
- Describe and compare the cultural characteristics of regions within India and evaluate their significance.

Competency goal 6

The learner will evaluate how Indians apply basic economic principles within community, state, and nation.

Objectives:

- Explain the relationship between unlimited wants and limited resources.
- Analyse the choices and opportunity cost involved in economic decisions.
- Categorise the state's resources as natural, human, or capital.
- Assess how state's natural resources are being used.
- Recognise that money can be used for spending, saving, and paying taxes.
- Analyse the relationship between government services and taxes.
- Describe the ways India specialises in economic activity and the relationship between specialisation and interdependence.
- Cite examples of interdependence in India's economy and evaluate the significance of economic relationships with other states and nations.

Competency goal 7

The learner will recognise how technology influences change within India.

Objectives:

- Cite examples from India's history of the impact of technology.

- Analyse the effect of technology on India's citizens, past and present.
- Explain how technology changed and influenced the movement of people, goods, and ideas over time.
- Analyse the effect of technology on Indian citizens today.
- Identify the advantages and disadvantages of technology in the lives of Indians.

Fifth Grade Study

The fifth grade study extends the focus to geographic regions of India, Pakistan, Bangladesh, and Sri Lanka, Nepal and Bhutan. Students learn about the people of these nations and the physical environments in which they live. As they examine social, economic, and political institutions, students analyse similarities and differences among societies. Concepts for this study are drawn from history and the social sciences, but the primary discipline is cultural geography.

Competency goal 1

The learner will apply key geographic concepts to India and other countries.

Objectives:

- Describe the absolute and relative location of major landforms, bodies of water, and natural resources in India and other countries of South Asia.
- Analyse how absolute and relative location influence ways of living in India and neighbouring countries.

- Compare and contrast the physical and cultural characteristics of regions within India and other countries of South Asia.
- Describe the economic and social differences between developed and developing regions in South Asia.
- Explain how and why population distribution differs within and between countries of South Asia.
- Explain how people of India and other countries of South Asia adapt to, modify, and use their physical environment.
- Analyse past movement of people, goods, and ideas within and among India and its neighbours and compare it to movement today.

Competency goal 2

The learner will analyse political and social institutions in South Asia and examine how these institutions respond to human needs, structure society, and influence behaviour.

Objectives:

- Analyse major documents that formed the foundations of the Indian idea of constitutional government.
- Describe the similarities and differences among the local, state, and national levels of government in India and explain their legislative, executive, and judicial functions.
- Recognise how Indian government has changed over time.
- Compare and contrast the government of India with the governments of neighbouring countries.

- Assess the role of political parties in society.
- Explain the role of public education in India.
- Compare and contrast the educational structure of India to selected countries of South Asia.
- Describe different types of families and compare and contrast the role the family plays in societal structures of India and selected countries of South Asia.

Competency goal 3

The learner will examine the roles various ethnic groups have played in the development of India and its neighbouring countries.

Objectives:

- Locate and describe people of diverse ethnic and religious cultures, past and present, in India.
- Examine how changes in the movement of people, goods, and ideas have affected ways of living in India.
- Identify examples of cultural interaction within and among the regions of India.
- Hypothesise how the differences and similarities among people have produced diverse Indian cultures.
- Describe the religious and ethnic impact of settlement on different regions of India.
- Describe art, music, and craft forms in India and compare them to various art forms in selected countries of South Asia.

Competency goal 4

The learner will trace key developments in Indian history

and describe their impact on the land and people of the nation and its neighbouring countries.

Objectives:

- Define the role of an historian and explain the importance of studying history.
- Explain when, where, why, and how groups of people settled in different regions of India.
- Describe the contributions of people of diverse cultures throughout the history of India.
- Evaluate the effectiveness of civil rights and social movements throughout India' history that reflect the struggle for equality and constitutional rights for all citizens.
- Compare and contrast changes in rural and urban settlement patterns in India, and other countries of South Asia.
- Trace the development of India as a world leader and analyse the impact of its relationships with neighbouring countries.

Competency goal 5

The learner will evaluate ways India and other countries of South Asia make decisions about the allocation and use of economic resources.

Objectives:

- Categorise economic resources found in India and neighbouring countries as human, natural, or capital and assess their long-term availability.
- Analyse the economic effects of the unequal distribution of natural resources on India and its neighbours.

- Assess economic institutions in terms of how well they enable people to meet their needs.
- Describe the ways in which the economies of India and its neighbours are interdependent and assess the impact of increasing international economic interdependence.
- Evaluate the influence of discoveries, inventions, and innovations on economic interdependence.
- Describe the ways India and its neighbours specialise in economic activities, and relate these to increased production and consumption.
- Cite examples of surplus and scarcity in the Indian market and explain the economic effects.

Competency goal 6

The learner will recognise how technology has influenced change within India and other countries in South Asia.

Objectives:

- Explore the meaning of technology as it encompasses discoveries from the first primitive tools to today's personal computer.
- Evaluate the effectiveness of civil rights and social movements throughout India' history that reflect the struggle for equality and constitutional rights for all citizens.
- Compare and contrast changes in rural and urban settlement patterns in India and other countries
- Trace the development of India as a world leader and analyse the impact of its relationships with other countries.

Secondary Level Teaching

At the secondary level, grades 9-12, students expand their understanding of history and the social sciences. The secondary level moves to a formal study of world and Indian history; links civics and economics in a course intended to provide students with the knowledge, skills, and attitudes to enter effectively into adult citizenship; and suggests a variety of social studies electives. While we cannot predict what specific knowledge and behaviour will be in demand as we venture in the twenty-first century, through social studies we can concentrate on educating citizens who will be scholarly, exercise leadership, and support democratic ideals.

We can prepare our students for a post secondary world, be it continued schooling or the workforce. The secondary level content sequence outlined is recommended, not required; however, there is a solid rationale for the specific suggested sequences. As students proceed from the study of World History through the study of Civics and Economics, concepts and generalisations develop the foundation for and contribute to more in-depth study of Indian History and the responsibilities of effective citizenship.

World History: The studies of World History in high school builds on the knowledge students have gained in the cultural geographic studies in grades five, six, and seven. Students emerge from a cultural geographic approach of the world to a more formal historical approach. World History examines the world chronologically and thematically, focusing on the historical development of phenomena, the rise and fall of civilisations and their unique contributions to humanity, and the universal elements these civilisations have in common throughout time. World History, recommended for grade nine, establishes the basis for the founding principles of Indian political and economic systems and democratic processes.

Civics and Economics: Through the study of Civics and Economics, students consider political, governmental, and legal topics that engage them in examining the legal and political systems of our society, and the basic economic concepts, economic institutions, as well as reasoned approaches for analysing economic problems, actions, and policies. Basic foundations in civics, government, and economics begin with and continue throughout the K-9 social studies programme. This course begins with the historical foundations of civil, political, and economic activism that created our nation, state, and localities. It empowers students to become politically and economically active and responsible citizens of the twenty-first century.

Indian History: The study of Indian History in high school builds on historical and geographical perspectives gained from the elementary and middle level study of India. The study of World History will enable students to place India in a world context. The economic and political perspectives and historical foundations gained from the study of Civics and Economics will prepare students for the examination of our nation's history. Given these foundational studies, it is appropriate that this high school course, Indian History, emphasises the economic, social, and political developments of the nation state up to and including the twentieth century.

The study of our nation's history concentrates on understanding cause-and-effect relationships and on developing an understanding of multiple causation, the knowledge that things are as they are for many reasons.

Such historical study leads beyond the memorisation of unexamined and isolated facts toward the ability to detect trends, analyse movements and events, and develop a "sense of history."

3

Teacher Performance

Constructivist Learning

A constructivist view of learning describes learning as an intellectual process in which learners develop what they know by fitting new ideas together with ideas they have already learned from previous experience, and they do this fitting together in their own unique ways. In the process of making these intellectual constructions, learners are influenced by the social and intellectual environments in which they find themselves. As a result, because much learning occurs in schools and classrooms, these settings affect both how and what learners learn. This constructivist learning process is often explained by using Jean Piaget's concepts of adaptation, assimilation, and accommodation.

When this explanation is provided in a school context, it can be described as follows: Learners see or hear something in their school environment (or experience it in some other way), interpret that new experience based on what they already know, and come to a personal understanding by connecting the new experience with their previous understanding. The result of the process is learning that is made up of three elements:

1) knowledge they gain from the new experience,
2) their prior understanding, and
3) their personal connection of the new and the old.

Because the learner's previous understanding is unique and because the intellectual process he or she uses to make the connections is unique as well, the construction is personally unique to each individual. Because learning occurs in this way, the primary teaching tasks of schools and teachers are to provide constructivist-rich learning experiences, to stimulate and guide learner constructivist thinking, and to remember continuously that all members of the community are learning all the time in their unique ways. Particularly important is the realisation that teachers continuously learn from and about students just as students learn from teachers.

The essential characteristics of powerful social studies consist of five principles and each principle has direct implications for what teachers should know and be able to do and what dispositions they should possess. The five principles are as follows:

1. *Social studies teaching and learning are powerful when they are meaningful.* Meaningfulness is stimulated when:
   - Students learn connected networks of knowledge, skills, beliefs, and attitudes that they will find useful both in and outside of school.
   - Instruction emphasises depth of development of important ideas within appropriate breadth of topic coverage and focuses on teaching these important ideas for understanding, appreciation, and life application.

- The significance and meaningfulness of the content is emphasised both in how it is presented to students and how it is developed through activities.
- Classroom interaction focuses on sustained examination of a few important topics rather than superficial coverage of many.
- Meaningful learning activities and assessment strategies focus students' attention on the most important ideas embedded in what they are learning.
- The teacher is reflective in planning, implementing, and assessing instruction.

2. *Social studies teaching and learning are powerful when they are integrative.* Integration is encouraged when:
   - Social studies subject matter is taught topically across disciplines.
   - The subject matter cuts across time and space.
   - The instruction interconnects knowledge, skills, beliefs, values, and attitudes to action.
   - The teaching makes effective use of technology.
   - Social studies teaching and learning are connected to other subjects.

3. *Social studies teaching and learning are powerful when they are values-based.* Social studies content invariably involves the examination and understanding of values—one's own and those of others—as values are expressed in points of view, beliefs, policies, actions, or inactions. Values-based instruction appropriate to education in a democratic society committed to safeguarding individual rights and the common good occurs when:

- Social studies teachers guide students to consider the ethical dimensions of topics and address controversial issues, providing an arena for reflective development of concern for the common good and application of social values.
- Students are made aware of potential social policy implications and taught to think critically and make value-based decisions about related social issues.
- Rather than promulgating personal, sectarian, or political views, teachers make sure that students: (a) become aware of the values, complexities, and dilemmas involved in an issue; (b) consider the costs and benefits to various individuals and groups that are embedded in potential courses of action; and (c) develop well-reasoned positions consistent with basic democratic social and political values.
- Teachers encourage recognition of opposing points of view, respect for well-supported positions, sensitivity to cultural similarities and differences, and a commitment to social responsibility.

4. *Social studies teaching and learning are powerful when they are challenging.* Social studies becomes challenging when:

   - Students are expected to strive to accomplish the instructional goals, both as individuals and group members.
   - Teachers model seriousness of purpose and a thoughtful approach to inquiry, and use instructional strategies designed to elicit and support similar qualities from students.
   - Teachers show interest in and respect for students' thinking and demand well-reasoned arguments

rather than opinions voiced without adequate thought or commitment.

5. *Social studies teaching and learning are powerful when the learning is active.* Social studies involves productive active learning when:
   - Teachers and students engage in reflective thinking and decision-making as events unfold during instruction.
   - Students develop new understanding through a process of active construction of knowledge.
   - Interactive discourse facilitates the construction of meaning required to develop important social understanding.
   - Teachers gradually move from providing considerable guidance by modelling, explaining, or supplying information that builds student knowledge, to a less directive role that encourages students to become independent and self-regulated learners. Teachers emphasise authentic activities that call for real-life applications using the skills and content of the field.

Subject Matter Standards

The subject matter standards are intended to assure that social studies teachers possess the knowledge, capabilities, and dispositions associated with the central concepts, tools of inquiry, and structures of the disciplines that make up the social studies and that they are able to create learning experiences that make these aspects of subject matter meaningful for learners. The subject matter standards are of three types: thematic standards, disciplinary standards, and programmatic standards for initial licensure. The thematic standards are based on the NCSS document *Expectations of Excellence: Curriculum Standards for Social Studies*, which describes NCSS expectations of what pre-K-12 learners should know and be able to do.

The thematic standards specify what social studies teachers should know and be able to do in order to teach the learners assigned to them. They apply to individuals, teacher preparation programmes, and state standards and procedures that concern licensure (or certification) for endorsement in (1) social studies as a broad field of endorsement; (2) any of the specific disciplines that fall within social studies—history, geography, civics and government, economics, psychology, sociology, and anthropology; and (3) other interdisciplinary licensure areas that are based primarily on social studies/social science subject matter.

The disciplinary standards are based on documents that have been compiled in recent years by various expert groups who have identified what they believe pre-K-12 learners should know and be able to do as a result of instruction in specific social studies/social science discipline-based subjects—history, geography, and so forth. The disciplinary standards specify what teachers in the specific licensure areas of history, geography, civics and government, economics, and psychology should know and be able to do to teach appropriately. Both the thematic and the disciplinary standards are expected to be used in four ways:

(1) to assess the knowledge and competence of individuals seeking licensure (or certification) to teach social studies or any of the disciplines within social studies,

(2) to assess the quality of teacher education programmes that prepare these individuals for initial licensure (or certification),

(3) to determine the appropriateness of state standards and procedures that are used to evaluate teacher preparation programmes that would be designated nationally approved by NCSS, and

(4) to guide those establishing criteria and procedures to be used for advanced certification of social studies teachers, such as the National Board for Professional Teaching Standards (NBPTS).

Although both sets of standards identify areas in which knowledge and competence are expected to be demonstrated, the standards do not specify minimums to be met. These standards stipulate what areas of knowledge and competence should be required of social studies teachers and the programmes that prepare them, and entities such as the institutions that prepare teachers, state licensure offices, the Interstate New Teacher Assistance and Support Consortium (INTASC), NCATE, NCSS reviewers of institutional programmes and state standards and procedures, and the NBPTS are expected to determine how much knowledge and competence is to be expected for each of the uses of the standards. It is realistic to assume that particularly well met standards will compensate in some degree for standards that are less well met.

The programmatic standards for initial licensure are of a different order from the thematic and disciplinary standards. They focus directly on teacher preparation programmes for initial licensure rather than on the individuals seeking the licenses. They are intended to assure that teacher preparation programmes provide the necessary experiences and resources to enable their teacher candidates to become knowledgeable and competent. They are expected to be used for NCSS approval of (1) institutional programmes and (2) state standards and procedures that are used to evaluate teacher preparation programmes that seek to be designated as nationally approved by NCSS.

Thematic Standards

The thematic standards apply to all individuals seeking initial licensure (or certification) in social studies, (1) as a broad field; (2) in any of the specific disciplines that fall within social studies—history, geography, civics and government, economics, psychology, sociology, and anthropology; and (3) in other interdisciplinary licensure areas that are based primarily on social studies/social science subject matter. They also apply to the teacher preparation programmes that prepare these individuals for these respective licenses (certificates). It is recognised however, that depths of knowledge and degrees of competence will, of necessity, vary across the ten standards from individual to individual and programme to programme.

Study of Culture and Cultural Diversity

Social studies teachers should possess the knowledge, capabilities, and dispositions to organise and provide instruction at the appropriate school level for the study of culture and cultural diversity.

Human beings create, learn, apply, modify, and adapt to their cultures. Culture helps them comprehend and make sense of themselves as individuals and members of various groups. Culture predisposes individuals to develop perspectives, make assumptions, create ideas, and behave in particular ways. Cultures tend to be similar in the ways they influence individuals and different in the specifics of the influence they have upon them. Therefore, the behaviours and products generated within and by cultures exhibit similarities and differences as well as some equivalences.

All cultures, for example, have systems of knowledge, values, traditions, and beliefs although the specifics of each may vary widely. Each cultural system is also unique. Cultures and each system within a culture are dynamic, ever-changing, and highly influential on the thoughts and actions of those who create them. In a democratic and culturally diverse society, students need to comprehend multiple perspectives that emerge from within their own culture and from the vantage points of the diverse cultural groups within that society and with whom the society may interact. These understandings allow them to make appropriate sense of the actions, ideas, and products of others as well as to relate to and interact with people within their diverse society and throughout the world.

Cultural diversity is a fact of existence in every modern-day society and few nations or empires in the past were void of such diversity. The challenge of all people is, wherever and whenever possible, to consider the strengths and advantages that this diversity offers to the society in general, and to their own growth as a human being in particular. This consideration is especially important in societies that value human rights, the principles of democracy and equity, as well as the notion that individuals should act to promote the public good.

Teachers of social studies at all school levels should provide developmentally appropriate experiences as they guide learners in the study of culture and cultural diversity. They should:

- enable learners to analyse and explain the ways groups, societies, and cultures address human needs and concerns;
- guide learners as they predict how data and experiences may be interpreted by people from diverse cultural perspectives and frames of reference;
- assist learners to apply an understanding of culture as an integrated whole that explains the functions and interactions of language, literature, the arts, traditions, beliefs and values, and behaviour patterns;
- encourage learners to compare and analyse societal patterns for preserving and transmitting culture while adapting to environmental or social change;
- enable learners to give examples and describe the importance of cultural unity and diversity within and across groups;
- have learners interpret patterns of behaviour reflecting values and attitudes that contribute or pose obstacles to cross-cultural understanding;
- guide learners as they construct reasoned judgments about specific cultural responses to persistent human issues;
- have learners explain and apply ideas, theories, and modes of inquiry drawn from anthropology and sociology in the examination of persistent issues and social problems.

In focusing on Culture and Cultural Diversity, teachers at various school levels should build upon learners' knowledge, experience, and developmental capabilities.

- Teachers of the early grades can assist learners to explore, comprehend, and apply critical information, ideas, and concepts that are common across societies, social institutions, cultures, and cultural perspectives. They can help learners comprehend cultural universals, such as norms, folkways, sanctions, social institutions, arts, and taboos and then use them to analyse their own and other cultures. They can use comparisons of cultures or subcultures and their perspectives, whether they exist in the present or past, to highlight contextual understanding. Socially, the young learner can be actively and frequently interacting in appropriate ways with other students, some of whom are like the learner and some different. These interactions can be encouraged and monitored and can involve rather than avoid dialogues about the substance of one's culture and perspectives.

– Teachers of the middle grades can assist learners to explore and ask questions about the nature of culture that provide a wider range of cultural universals and in-depth study of the specific aspects of particular cultures in similar and different places, times, conditions, and contexts. Teachers can encourage learners to consider the direct and indirect connections between the assumptions, beliefs, and values of a culture and its actions, policies, and products in multiple situations. They can help them analyse the ways that a people's cultural ideas and actions influence its members. Through this inquiry, learners can begin to consider such phenomena as cultural lag, assimilation, accommodation, and the strength of the impact traditions have on thought and action within any particular social group.

– High school teachers can assist learners to deepen their comprehension and increase their application of cultural concepts already studied, such as cultural lag, assimilation, accommodation, and the impact of traditions on thought and action within any particular social group. They can also introduce new concepts such as the function and interactions of language, literature, and the arts in terms of traditions, beliefs, and values; and the transmitting of culture in the face of environmental, technical, and social change. Learners should be able to engage independently in in-depth analysis of any cultural group or subgroup and in-depth comparison of any two or more cultural groups or subgroups. They should be able to connect their comprehension of cultural groups to the realities of cultural diversity within multicultural societies and consider how culturally different groups can cooperate to enhance the public good.

Study of Time, Continuity, and Change

Social studies teachers should possess the knowledge, capabilities, and dispositions to organise and provide instruction at the appropriate school level for the study of Time, Continuity, and Change. The study of time, continuity, and change allows learners to understand their historical roots and to locate themselves in time. Learning how to read and reconstruct the past allows them to develop a historical perspective and to answer questions such as: Who am I? What happened in the past? How has the world changed and how might it change in the future? Why does our personal sense of relatedness to the past change? How can the perspective we have about our own life experiences be viewed as part of the larger human story across time? How do our personal stories reflect varying points of view and inform contemporary ideas and actions? Learners also draw on their knowledge of history to make informed choices and decisions in the present.

Teachers of social studies at all school levels should provide developmentally appropriate experiences as they guide learners in the study of time, continuity, and change. They should:

- assist learners to understand that historical knowledge and the concept of time are socially influenced constructions that lead historians to be selective in the questions they seek to answer and the evidence they use;
- help learners apply key concepts such as time, chronology, causality, change, conflict, and complexity to explain, analyse, and show connections among patterns of historical change and continuity;
- enable learners to identify and describe significant historical periods and patterns of change within and across cultures, such as the development of ancient cultures and civilisations, the rise of nation-states, and social, economic, and political revolutions;
- guide learners as they systematically employ processes of critical historical inquiry to reconstruct and interpret the past, such as using a variety of sources and checking their credibility, validating and weighing evidence for claims, and searching for causality;
- provide learners with opportunities to investigate, interpret, and analyse multiple historical and contemporary viewpoints within and across cultures related to important events, recurring dilemmas, and persistent issues, while employing empathy, skepticism, and critical judgment; enable learners to apply ideas, theories, and modes of historical inquiry to analyse historical and contemporary developments, and to inform and evaluate actions concerning public policy issues.

In focusing on the theme Time, Continuity, and Change, teachers at various school levels should build upon learners' knowledge, experience, and developmental capabilities.

- Teachers of the early grades can provide learners experience with sequencing to help establish a sense of order and time. Teachers at this level can make stories of the recent past as well as of long ago available to learners. In addition, they can begin to help learners recognise that individuals may hold different views about the past and understand the linkages between human decisions and consequences. Teachers of these grades can lay the foundation for the development of historical knowledge, skills, and values.
- Teachers of the middle grades can provide a beginning level of a formal study of history so that learners can continue to expand their understanding of the past and of historical concepts and inquiry. At this level, teachers can facilitate the understanding and appreciation of differences in historical perspectives, and the recognition that interpretations are influenced by individual experiences, societal values, and cultural traditions.
- High school teachers can engage learners in a sophisticated analysis and reconstruction of the past, helping them to examine the relationship of the past to the present and extrapolating into the future. Teachers can facilitate learners' integration of individual stories about people, events, and situations so that they might form a holistic conception, in which continuity and change are linked in time and across cultures. Teachers can help learners to draw on their knowledge of history to make informed choices and decisions in the present.

Study of People, Places, and Environments

Social studies teachers should possess the knowledge, capabilities, and dispositions to organise and provide instruction at the appropriate school level for the study of People, Places, and Environments. The study of people, places, and human-environment interactions leads learners to create their spatial views and geographic perspectives of the world. Today's social, cultural, economic, and civic demands on individuals require that learners understand the world in spatial terms and possess knowledge of places and regions, physical systems, and the interactions of environment and society.

In addition, learners need the ability to map information in a spatial context and to interpret such maps. The study of people, places, and environments will also help to promote learners' capabilities to make informed and critical decisions about the relationships between human beings and their environment. Teachers of social studies at all school levels should provide developmentally appropriate experiences as they guide learners in the study of people, places, and environments. They should

- enable learners to construct, use, and refine mental maps of locales, regions, and the world that demonstrate their understanding of relative location, direction, size, and shape;
- have learners create, interpret, use, and distinguish various representations of Earth, such as maps, globes, and photographs, and use appropriate geographic tools such as atlases, data bases, systems, charts, graphs, and maps to generate, manipulate, and interpret information;

- teach learners to estimate and calculate distance, scale, area, and density, and to distinguish spatial distribution patterns;
- help learners to locate, distinguish, and describe the relationships among varying regional and global patterns of geographic phenomena such as landforms, climate, and natural resources;
- challenge learners to speculate about and explain physical system changes, such as seasons, climate, and weather;
- help learners describe how people create places that reflect culture, human needs, current values and ideals, and government policies;
- challenge learners to examine, interpret, and analyse the interactions of human beings and their physical environments;
- have learners explore the ways Earth's physical features have changed over time; and describe and assess the ways historical events have influenced and have been influenced by physical and human geographic features;
- provide learners with opportunities to observe and analyse social and economic effects of environmental changes and crises;
- challenge learners to consider, compare, and evaluate existing alternative uses of resources and land in communities, regions, nations, and the world.

In focusing on the theme People, Places, and Environments, teachers at various school levels should build upon learners' knowledge, experience, and developmental capabilities.

- Teachers of the early grades can use learners' immediate personal experiences to have them reflect upon elements in their environment and how we use and think about the physical and built environment. They can also stimulate learners' interest in things distant and unfamiliar and help lay the foundation for concern about the use and abuse of the physical environment.
- Teachers of the middle grades can help learners relate their personal experiences to happenings in other environmental contexts. They can provide learning experiences which encourage increasingly abstract thought as learners use data and apply skills in analysing human behaviour in relation to its physical and cultural environments.
- High school teachers can guide learners in the application of geographic understandings across a broad range of fields, including the fine arts, science, and the humanities. They can facilitate the expansion of diverse cultures, both historical and contemporary, so the geographic concepts become central to the learners' comprehension of global connections. They can also help learners recognise the importance of core geographic concepts to public policy and enable learners to address issues of domestic and international significance.

Study of Individual Development and Identity

Social studies teachers should possess the knowledge, capabilities, and dispositions to organise and provide instruction at the appropriate school level for the study of Individual Development and Identity.

All humans think, learn, act, and develop cognitively, socially, physically, emotionally, personally, and mentally as well as construct, test, confirm, revise, and apply multiple concepts of and multiple identities as to who they are. While much of what humans are and become has been associated with genetics and assumed natural stages of physical, psychological, emotional, and mental development, a far greater factor in mental, social, emotional, personal, and identity construction and application is the interaction of the individual with his or her environments and the consequences of these interactions. All individuals should know the factors that contribute to who they are; to what they think, feel, and believe; to what they decide and do; to why they are likely to make certain decisions and act in particular ways; and to how they perceive themselves, their abilities, their personality, and the world.

Teachers of social studies at all school levels should provide developmentally appropriate experiences as they guide learners in the study of ideas associated with individual human development and identity. They should

- assist learners in articulating personal connections to time, place, and social/cultural systems;
- help learners to identify, describe, and express appreciation for the influences of various historical and contemporary cultures on an individual's daily life;
- assist learners to describe the ways family, religion, gender, ethnicity, nationality, socioeconomic status, and other group and cultural influences contribute to the development of a sense of self;
- have learners apply concepts, methods, and theories about the study of human growth and development, such as physical endowment, learning, motivation, behaviour, perception, and personality;

- guide learners as they examine the interactions of ethnic, national, or cultural influences in specific situations or events;
- enable learners to analyse the role of perceptions, attitudes, values, and beliefs in the development of personal identity;
- have learners compare and evaluate the impact of stereotyping, conformity, acts of altruism, and other behaviours on individuals and groups;
- assist learners as they work independently and cooperatively within groups and institutions to accomplish goals;
- enable learners to examine factors that contribute to and damage one's mental health and analyse issues related to mental health and behavioural disorders in contemporary society.

Study of Individuals, Groups, and Institutions

Social studies teachers should possess the knowledge, capabilities, and dispositions to organise and provide instruction at the appropriate school level for the study of interactions among Individuals, Groups, and Institutions.

Institutions such as schools, churches, families, government agencies, and the courts all play integral roles in our lives. These and other institutions exert enormous influence over us, yet institutions are no more than organisational embodiments to further the core social values of those who comprise them. Thus, it is important that learners know how institutions are formed, what controls and influences them, how they control and influence individuals and culture, and how institutions can be maintained or changed. The study of individuals, groups, and institutions, drawing upon sociology, anthropology, and other disciplines, prepares learners to ask and answer questions such as: What is the role of institutions in this and other societies? How am I influenced by institutions? How do institutions change? What is my role in institutional change?

Teachers of social studies at all school levels should provide developmentally appropriate experiences as they guide learners in the study of interactions among individuals, groups, and institutions. They should

- help learners understand the concepts of role, status, and social class and use them in describing the connections and interactions of individuals, groups, and institutions in society;
- help learners analyse group and institutional influences on people, events, and elements of culture in both historical and contemporary settings;
- explain to learners the various forms institutions take, and explain how they develop and change over time;
- assist learners in identifying and analysing examples of tensions between expressions of individuality and efforts used to promote social conformity by groups and institutions;
- enable learners to describe and examine belief systems basic to specific traditions and laws in contemporary and historical movements;
- challenge learners to evaluate the role of institutions in furthering both continuity and change;
- guide learner analysis of the extent to which groups and institutions meet individual needs and promote

the common good in contemporary and historical settings;

- assist learners as they explain and apply ideas and modes of inquiry drawn from behavioral science and social theory in the examination of persistent social issues and problems.

Study of Power, Authority, and Governance

Social studies teachers should possess the knowledge, capabilities, and dispositions to organise and provide instruction at the appropriate school level for the study of Power, Authority, and Governance.

Understanding the historical development of structures of power, authority, and governance and their evolving functions in contemporary American society, as well as in other parts of the world, is essential for the development in learners of civic competence. In exploring this theme, learners confront such questions as: What is power? What is legitimate authority? How are governments created, structured, maintained, and changed? How can we keep government responsive to its citizens' needs and interests? How can individual rights be protected within the context of majority rule?

By examining the characteristics of various governance systems, learners develop an understanding of how groups and nations attempt to resolve conflicts and seek to establish order and security. Through study of dynamic relationships among individual rights and responsibilities, the needs of social groups, and concepts of a just society, learners become more effective problem solvers and decision-makers when addressing persistent social problems encountered in public life.

Teachers of social studies at all school levels should provide developmentally appropriate experiences as they guide learners in the study of power, authority, and governance. They should

- enable learners to examine the rights and responsibilities of the individual in relation to his or her family, social groups, community, and nation;
- help students to understand the purpose of government and how its powers are acquired, used, and justified;
- provide opportunities for learners to examine issues involving the rights, roles, and status of individuals in relation to the general welfare;
- enable learners to describe the ways nations and organisations respond to forces of unity and diversity affecting order and security;
- have learners explain conditions, actions, and motivations that contribute to conflict and cooperation within and among nations;
- help learners to analyse and explain governmental mechanisms to meet the needs and wants of citizens, regulate territory, manage conflict, and establish order and security;
- have learners identify and describe the basic features of the American political system, and identify representative leaders from various levels and branches of government;
- challenge learners to apply concepts such as power, role, status, justice, and influence to the examination of persistent issues and social problems;

– guide learners to explain how governments attempt to achieve their stated ideals at home and abroad.

Production, Distribution, and Consumption of Goods

Social studies teachers should possess the knowledge, capabilities, and dispositions to organise and provide instruction at the appropriate school level for the study of how people organise for the Production, Distribution, and Consumption of goods and services.

People have wants that often exceed the limited resources available to them, and as a result, they have invented a variety of ways to decide upon answers to four fundamental questions: What is to be produced? How is production to be organised? How are goods and services to be distributed? What is the most effective allocation of the factors of production (land, labour, capital, and management)? Learners need to understand these questions and how they are being addressed by various groups. They also need to understand that unequal distribution of resources necessitates systems of exchange, including trade, to improve the well-being of individual groups, and the economy; that the role of government in economic policy-making varies over time and from place to place; that increasingly economic decisions are global in scope and require systematic study of an interdependent world economy; and that technology plays a significant role in economic decision-making.

Teachers of social studies at all school levels should provide developmentally appropriate experiences as they guide learners in the study of how people organise for the production, distribution, and consumption of goods and services. They should

- enable learners to explain how the scarcity of productive resources (human, capital, technological, and natural) requires the development of economic systems to make decisions about how goods and services are to be produced and distributed;
- help learners analyse the role that supply and demand, prices, incentives, and profits play in determining what is produced and distributed in a competitive market system;
- help learners compare the costs and benefits to society of allocating goods and services through private and public means;
- assist learners to see the relationships among the various economic institutions that comprise economic systems such as households, businesses, banks, government agencies, labor unions, and corporations;
- guide learner analysis of the role of specialisation and exchange in economic processes;
- provide opportunities for learners to assess how values and beliefs influence economic decisions in different societies;
- have learners compare basic economic systems according to how rules and procedures deal with demand, supply, prices, the role of government, banks, labor and labor unions, savings and investments, and capital;
- challenge learners to apply economic concepts and reasoning when evaluating historical and contemporary social developments and issues;
- enable learners to distinguish between the domestic and global economic systems, and explain how the two interact;

- guide learners in the application of knowledge of production, distribution, and consumption in the analysis of public issues such as the allocation of health care or the consumption of energy, and in devising economic plans for accomplishing socially desirable outcomes related to such issues;
- help learners to distinguish between economics as a field of inquiry and the economy.

Study of Science, Technology, and Society

Social studies teachers should possess the knowledge, capabilities, and dispositions to organise and provide instruction at the appropriate school level for the study of science, technology, and society.

Science is an enterprise that focuses on inquiry about natural phenomena; technology is the designing of things and processes to achieve practical purposes. Learners need to realise that both science and technology have had a profound effect in shaping human experience and the world around us. Tracing the impact of science and technology in such areas of human endeavor as agriculture, manufacturing, the production and distribution of goods and services, the use of energy, communication, transportation, information processing, medicine and health care, and warfare enables learners to understand both the way science and technology have influenced and have been influenced by individuals, societies, and cultures. By examining questions and issues raised historically and contemporaneously resulting from scientific inquiry and technological applications, learners can be better prepared to make informed decisions as citizens about individual choices and policy alternatives that face society.

Teachers of social studies at all school levels should provide developmentally appropriate experiences as they guide learners in the study of science and technology. They should

- enable learners to identify, describe, and examine both current and historical examples of the interaction and interdependence of science, technology, and society in a variety of cultural settings;
- provide opportunities for learners to make judgments about how science and technology have transformed the physical world and human society and understanding of time, space, place, and human-environment interactions;
- have learners analyse the way in which science and technology influence core societal values, beliefs, and attitudes and how societal attitudes shape scientific and technological change;
- prompt learners to evaluate various policies proposed to deal with social changes resulting from new technologies;
- help learners to identify and interpret various perspectives about human societies and the physical world using scientific knowledge, technologies, and ethical standards from diverse world cultures;
- encourage learners to formulate strategies and develop policy proposals for influencing public discussions associated with science/technology-society issues.

Study of Global Connections and Interdependence

Social studies teachers should possess the knowledge, capabilities, and dispositions to provide instruction at the appropriate school level for the study of Global Connections and Interdependence. The realities of global interdependence require that learners understand the increasingly important and diverse global connections among world societies. Analysis of tensions between national interests and global priorities contributes to the development of possible solutions to persistent and emerging global issues in many fields: health care, economic development, environmental quality, universal human rights, and others. Analysing patterns and relationships within and among world cultures, such as economic competition and interdependence, age-old ethnic enmities, political and military alliances, and others, helps learners examine policy alternatives that have both national and global implications.

Teachers of social studies at all school levels should provide developmentally appropriate experiences as they guide learners in the study of global connections and interdependence. They should

- enable learners to explain how language, art, music, belief systems, and other cultural elements can facilitate global understanding or cause misunderstanding;
- help learners to explain conditions and motivations that contribute to conflict, cooperation, and interdependence among groups, societies, and nations;
- provide opportunities for learners to analyse and evaluate the effects of changing technologies on the global community;
- challenge learners to analyse the causes, consequences, and possible solutions to persistent, contemporary, and emerging global issues, such as health care, security,

resource allocation, economic development, and environmental quality;

- guide learner analysis of the relationships and tensions between national sovereignty and global interests in such matters as territorial disputes, economic development, nuclear and other weapons deployment, use of natural resources, and human rights concerns;
- have learners analyse or formulate policy statements in such ways that they demonstrate an understanding of concerns, standards, issues, and conflicts related to universal human rights;
- help learners to describe and evaluate the role of international and multinational organisations in the global arena;
- have learners illustrate how individual behaviours and decisions connect with global systems.

Study of Civic Ideals and Practices

Social studies teachers should possess the knowledge, capabilities, and dispositions to organise and provide instruction at the appropriate school level for the study of Civic Ideals and Practices.

The study of civic ideals and practices prepares learners for full participation in society and is a central purpose of the social studies. Examining civic ideals and practices across time and in diverse societies prepares learners to close the gap between present practices and the ideals upon which our democratic republic is based. Learners confront such questions as: What is civic participation and how can I be involved? How has the meaning of citizenship evolved? What is the balance between rights and responsibilities? What is the role of the citizen in the community, in the nation, and in the world community? How can I make a positive difference?

Teachers of social studies at all school levels should provide developmentally appropriate experiences as they guide learners in the study of civic ideals and practices. They should

- assist learners to understand the origins and interpret the continuing influence of key ideals of the democratic republican form of government, such as individual human dignity, liberty, justice, equality, and the rule of law;
- guide learner efforts to identify, analyse, interpret, and evaluate sources and examples of citizens' rights and responsibilities;
- facilitate learner efforts to locate, access, analyse, organise, synthesise, evaluate, and apply information about selected public issues—identifying, describing, and evaluating multiple points of view;
- provide opportunities for learners to practice forms of civic discussion and participation consistent with the ideals of citizens in a democratic republic;
- help learners to analyse and evaluate the influence of various forms of citizen action on public policy;
- prepare learners to analyse a variety of public policies and issues from the perspective of formal and informal political actors;
- guide learners as they evaluate the effectiveness of public opinion in influencing and shaping public policy development and decision-making;
- encourage learner efforts to evaluate the degree to which public policies and citizen behaviours reflect or

foster the stated ideals of a democratic republican form of government;

- support learner efforts to construct policy statements and action plans to achieve goals related to issues of public concern;
- create opportunities for learner participation in activities to strengthen the "common good," based upon careful evaluation of possible options for citizen action.

The disciplinary standards apply respectively to individuals seeking initial licensure (or certification) in each of the social studies discipline areas of history, geography, civics and government, economics, and psychology as well as to the teacher preparation programmes that prepare them for these licenses. Although these standards should be considered the primary standards for the subject matter component of each discipline-based license, the individuals seeking these licenses and their teacher preparation programmes are also expected to meet the ten thematic standards described above. It is recognised, however, that, because of the discipline focus of these licenses, the depth of knowledge and degrees of competence across the ten thematic standards will vary and will likely be less substantial than for those seeking endorsement in social studies as a broad field.

Teaching History

Teachers who are licensed to teach history at all school levels should possess the knowledge, capabilities, and dispositions to organise and provide instruction at the appropriate school level for the study of history.

The study of history allows learners to understand their place in time and location. The knowledge base of historical content drawn from United States and world history provides the basis from which learners develop historical understanding and competence in ways of historical thinking. Historical thinking skills enable learners to evaluate evidence, develop comparative and causal analyses, interpret the historical record, and construct sound historical arguments and perspectives on which informed decisions in contemporary life can be based.

Historical understandings define what learners should know about the history of their nation and of the world. These understandings are drawn from the record of human aspirations, strivings, accomplishments, and failures in at least five spheres of human activity: the social, political, scientific/technological, economic, and cultural (philosophical/religious/aesthetic). They also provide learners the historical perspectives necessary to analyse contemporary issues and problems confronting citizens today.

Teachers of history at all school levels should provide developmentally appropriate experiences as they guide learners in their study. They should

- assist learners in utilising chronological thinking so that they can distinguish between past, present, and future time; can place historical narratives in the proper chronological framework; can interpret data presented in time lines; and can compare alternative models for periodisation;
- enable learners to develop historical comprehension in order that they might reconstruct the literal meaning of a historical passage, identify the central question(s) addressed in historical narrative, draw upon data in historical maps, charts, and other graphic organisers; and draw upon visual, literary, or musical sources;

- guide learners in practicing skills of historical analysis and interpretation, such as compare and contrast, differentiate between historical facts and interpretations, consider multiple perspectives, analyse cause and effect relationships, compare competing historical narratives, recognise the tentative nature of historical interpretations, and hypothesise the influence of the past;
- assist learners in developing historical research capabilities that enable them to formulate historical questions, obtain historical data, question historical data, identify the gaps in available records, place records in context, and construct sound historical interpretations;
- help learners to identify issues and problems in the past, recognise factors contributing to such problems, identify and analyse alternative courses of action, formulate a position or course of action, and evaluate the implementation of that decision;
- assist learners in acquiring knowledge of historical content in United States history in order to ask large and searching questions that compare patterns of continuity and change in the history and values of the many peoples who have contributed to the development of the continent of North America;
- guide learners in acquiring knowledge of the history and values of diverse civilisations throughout the world, including those of the West, and in comparing patterns of continuity and change in different parts of the world;
- enable learners to develop historical understanding through the avenues of social, political, economic, and

cultural history and the history of science and technology.

Teaching Geography

Teachers who are licensed to teach geography at all school levels should possess the knowledge, capabilities, and dispositions to organise and provide instruction at the appropriate school level for the study of geography.

The study of geography allows learners to develop an understanding of the spatial contexts of people, places, and environments. It provides knowledge of Earth's physical and human systems and the interdependency of living things and physical environments. Studying geography stimulates curiosity about the world and the world's diverse inhabitants and places, as well as about local, regional, and global issues. Geography allows learners to understand and make decisions about issues at the global as well as the local level.

Teachers of geography at all school levels should provide developmentally appropriate experiences as they guide learners in their study. They should

- guide learners in the use of maps and other geographic representations, tools, and technologies to acquire, process, and report information from a spatial perspective;
- enable learners to use mental maps to organise information about people, places, and environments in a spatial context;
- assist learners to analyse the spatial information about people, places, and environments on Earth's surface;
- help learners to understand the physical and human characteristics of places;
- assist learners in developing the concept of regions as a means to interpret Earth's complexity;

- enable learners to understand how culture and experience influence people's perceptions of places and regions;
- provide learners opportunities to understand and analyse the physical processes that shape Earth's surface;
- challenge learners to consider the characteristics and spatial distribution of ecosystems on Earth's surface;
- guide learners in exploring the characteristics, distribution, and migration of human populations on Earth's surface;
- help learners to understand and analyse the characteristics, distribution, and complexity of Earth's cultural mosaics;
- have learners explore the patterns and networks of economic interdependence on Earth's surface;
- enable learners to describe the processes, patterns, and functions of human settlement;
- challenge learners to examine how the forces of cooperation and conflict among people influence the division and control of Earth's surface;
- help learners see how human actions modify the physical environment;
- enable learners to analyse how physical systems affect human systems;
- challenge learners to examine the changes that occur in the meaning, use, distribution, and importance of resources;
- help learners to apply geography to interpret the past and present and to plan for the future;

- enhance learners' abilities to ask questions and to acquire, organise, and analyse geographic information so they can answer geographic questions as they engage in the study of substantive geographic content.

Teaching Civics and Government

Teachers who are licensed to teach civics and/or government at all school levels should possess the knowledge, capabilities, and dispositions to organise and provide instruction at the appropriate school level for the study of civics and government.

The goal of education in civics and government is informed, responsible participation in political life by competent citizens committed to the fundamental values and principles of American constitutional democracy. This effective and responsible participation requires the acquisition of a body of knowledge and of intellectual and participatory skills. Effective and responsible participation also is furthered by the development of certain dispositions or traits of character that enhance the individual's capacity to participate in the political process and contribute to the healthy functioning of the political system and improvement of society.

Teachers of civics and government at all school levels should provide developmentally appropriate experiences as they guide learners in their study. They should

- assist learners in developing an understanding of civic life, politics, and government, so that the learners can explore the origins of governmental authority, recognise the need for government; identify the crucial functions of government, including laws and rules; evaluate rules and laws; differentiate between limited and unlimited government; and appreciate the importance of limitations on government power;

- guide learners as they explore American democracy, including the American idea of constitutional government, the impact of the distinctive characteristics of American society on our government, the nature of the American political culture, and the values and principles that are basic to American life and government;
- help learners understand how the government of the United States operates under the constitution and the purposes, values, and principles of American democracy, including the ideas of distributed, shared, and limited powers of government; how the national, state, and local governments are organised; and the place of law in the system;
- enable learners to understand the relationship of the United States to other nations and to world affairs;
- assist learners in developing an understanding of citizenship, its rights and responsibilities, and in developing their abilities and dispositions to participate effectively in civic life.
- insure that learners are made aware of the full range of opportunities to participate as citizens in the American democracy and of their responsibilities for doing so.

Teaching Economics

Teachers who are licensed to teach economics at all school levels should possess the knowledge, capabilities, and dispositions to organise and provide instruction at the appropriate school level for the study of economics.

The study of economics provides learners with basic information about how people attempt to satisfy their wants and helps them employ logical reasoning in thinking about economic issues. It enables them to understand the economic issues that affect them every day, the roles they play as consumers and producers, and the costs and benefits associated with their personal decisions as well as governmental practice.

Teachers of economics at all school levels should provide developmentally appropriate experiences as they guide learners in their study. They should assist learners in acquiring an understanding of the following principles:

- Productive resources are limited. Therefore, people cannot have all the goods and services that they want; as a result, they must choose some things and give up others.
- Effective decision making requires comparing the additional costs of alternatives with the additional benefits. Most choices involve doing a little more or a little less of something; few choices are all or nothing decisions.
- Different methods can be used to allocate goods and services. People, acting individually or collectively through government, must choose which methods to use to allocate different kinds of goods and services.
- People respond predictably to positive and negative incentives.
- Voluntary exchange occurs only when all parties expect to gain. This is true for trade among individuals or organisations within a nation, or among individuals or organisations in different nations.

When individuals, regions, and nations specialise in what they can produce at the lowest cost and then trade with others, both production and consumption increase.

- Markets exist when buyers and sellers interact. This interaction determines market prices and thereby allocates scarce goods and services.
- Prices send signals and provide incentives to buyers and sellers. When supply and demand change, market prices adjust, affecting incentives.
- Competition among sellers lowers costs and prices, encouraging producers to produce more of what consumers are willing and able to buy. Competition among buyers increases prices and allocates goods and services to those people who are willing and able to pay the most for them.
- Institutions evolve in market economies to help individuals and groups accomplish their goals. Banks, labor unions, corporations, legal systems, and not-for-profit organisations are examples of important institutions. A different kind of institution, clearly defined and enforced property rights, is essential to a market economy.
- Money makes it easier to trade, borrow, save, invest, and compare the value of goods and services.
- Interest rates, adjusted for inflation, rise and fall to balance the amount saved with the amount borrowed, thus affecting the allocation of scarce resources between present and future users.
- Income for most people is determined by the market value of the productive resources they sell. What

workers earn depends, primarily, on the market value of what they produce and how productive they are.

- Entrepreneurs are people who take the risks of organising productive resources to make goods and services. Profit is an important incentive that leads entrepreneurs to accept the risks of business failure.
- Investment in factories, machinery, new technology, and in the health, education, and training of people can raise future standards of living.
- There is an economic role for government to play in a market economy whenever the benefits of a government policy outweigh its costs. Governments often provide for national defence, address environmental concerns, define and protect property rights, and attempt to make markets more competitive. Most government policies also redistribute income.
- Costs of government policies sometimes exceed benefits. This may occur because of incentives facing voters, government officials, and government employees; because of actions by special interest groups that can impose costs on the general public; or because social goals other than economic efficiency are being pursued.
- A nation's overall levels of income, employment, and prices are determined by the interaction of spending and production decisions made by all households, firms, government agencies, and others in the economy.
- Unemployment imposes costs on individuals and nations. Unexpected inflation imposes costs on many people and benefits some others because it arbitrarily redistributes purchasing power. Inflation can reduce

the rate of growth of national living standards because individuals and organisations use resources to protect themselves against the uncertainty of future prices.

Teaching Psychology

Teachers who are licensed to teach psychology at all school levels should possess the knowledge, capabilities, and dispositions to organise and provide instruction at the appropriate school level for the study of psychology. The study of psychology and human behaviour allows learners to understand major theories that have been proposed to describe human thinking, learning, memory, development, personality, and behaviour.

Teachers of psychology at all school levels should provide developmentally appropriate experiences as they guide learners in their study. They should:

- assist learners in comprehending and applying concepts, theories, and principles associated with human cognition; emotional, social, and personal development; and growth and change;
- guide learner understanding of human thinking, memory, perception, learning, development, and behaviour;
- assist learner comprehension of factors associated with human adjustment and coping behaviours in various situations, during different stages of life, and in respect to particular personal and environmental situations;
- have learners consider how such factors as memory, thinking, beliefs, emotions, personality, perceptions, attitude, and abilities may affect their decisions and actions at any particular moment and may be used to

interpret and comprehend possible decisions and actions by others;

- have learners examine factors associated with the construction, revision, and use of self-concepts and identity and how these may affect an individual's thinking, feelings, decisions, and actions toward self, others, and the world;
- have learners examine factors that may have contributed to their own self-concepts and identity, including how their family, groups, peers, and communities may have contributed;
- have learners examine and comprehend factors associated with personality and individual differences and how personality and these differences have been and may be described, classified, assessed, and interpreted;
- assist learners to examine, comprehend, and apply ideas associated with mental and emotional health as well as psychological disorders, including factors contributing to and the treatment of such disorders;
- enable learners to understand interconnections between themselves and particular situations, places, time, events, and social/cultural environments and systems that may influence them as well as be influenced by them;
- insure that learners comprehend, consider the advantages and disadvantages of, and apply concepts, principles, and procedures for conducting, monitoring, applying, and interpreting sound psychology research activities;
- insure that learners consider the various codes of ethics accepted by psychologists regarding the conducting of

research on human and animal subjects and the reporting of research findings;

- enable students to engage in preliminary behavioral science research, using various research paradigms and perspectives.

4

Effective Teaching of Social Science

Powerful social studies teaching helps students develop social understanding and civic efficacy. Social understanding is integrated knowledge of social aspects of the human condition: how they have evolved over time, the variations that occur in various physical environments and cultural settings, and the emerging trends that appear likely to shape the future. Civic efficacy—the readiness and willingness to assume citizenship responsibilities—is rooted in social studies knowledge and skills, along with related values (such as concern for the common good) and attitudes (such as an orientation toward participation in civic affairs).

The nation depends on a well-informed and civic-minded citizenry to sustain its democratic traditions, especially now as it adjusts to its own heterogeneous society and its shifting roles in an increasingly interdependent and changing world. There is a need for a guiding vision to assist social studies teachers in planning their instruction and focusing their students' learning. This need is derived from two features of social studies that distinguish it from other school subjects and provide special instructional challenges.

First, social studies is diverse, encompassing a great ınge of potential content. When taught well, its content is rawn not only from its most direct foundational disciplines ıt also from the arts and humanities, mathematics and :ience, current events, and students' own interests and ‹periences. This content, however, is not treated simply as ‿ollections of miscellaneous information and activities, but rather is organised within a coherent citizen education curriculum.

Second, the social understanding and civic efficacy goals of social studies place special responsibilities on teachers for addressing the ethical and social policy aspects of topics. When taught well, social studies engages students in the difficult process of confronting ethical and value-based dilemmas, and encourages students to speculate, think critically, and make personal and civic decisions based on information from multiple perspectives.

Powerful social studies teaching begins with a clear understanding of the subject's unique purposes and goals. The US National Council for the Social Studies' (NCSS) statement "Essentials of the Social Studies" identifies citizenship education as the primary purpose of K-12 social studies. Noting that concern for the common good and citizen participation in public life are essential to the health of our democratic system, it states that effective social studies programmes prepare young people to identify, understand, and work to solve the problems facing our diverse nation in an increasingly interdependent world. Such programmes:

- foster individual and cultural identity along with understanding of the forces that hold society together or pull it apart;

- include observation of and participation in the school and community;
- address critical issues and the world as it is;
- prepare students to make decisions based on democratic principles; and
- lead to citizen participation in public affairs.

Curriculum components include knowledge, democratic values and beliefs, thinking skills, and social and civic participation skills. Knowledge refers to interpretations that students construct in response to their experiences in and out of school. Knowledge is not merely a fixed body of information transmitted for students to memorise. Teachers should not only expose their students to curriculum content but should also provide them with opportunities to think and communicate in ways that will help students construct a working knowledge of such content.

The content of social studies focuses on the world—near and far, social and civic, past, present, and future. Effective social studies teaching draws this content from the social studies foundational disciplines (such as geography, government, and history) and links it with knowledge that students have acquired through life experiences and the media. It builds knowledge about the history and cultures of our nation and the world, geographical relationships, economic systems and processes, social and political institutions, interpersonal and intergroup relations, and worldwide relationships among nations, races, cultures, and institutions. From this knowledge base, exemplary programmes help students to:

(1) develop skills, concepts, and generalisations necessary to understand the sweep of human affairs:

(2) appreciate the benefits of diversity and community, the value of widespread economic opportunity, and the contributions that people of both genders and the full range of ethnic, racial, and religious groups have made to our society;

(3) become ready and willing to contribute to public policy formulation; and

(4) acquire ways of managing conflict that are consistent with democratic procedures.

The fundamental values and beliefs taught in social studies are drawn from many sources, but especially from the Declaration of Independence and the United States Constitution with its Bill of Rights. These beliefs form the basic principles of our democratic constitutional order. They depend on such practices as due process, equal protection, free expression, and civic participation, and they have roots in the concepts of liberty, justice, equality, responsibility, diversity, and privacy. Exemplary programmes do not indoctrinate students to accept these ideas blindly. Instead, they present knowledge about their historical derivation and contemporary application necessary to understand our society and its institutions.

Teachers model fundamental democratic principles in their classrooms, discuss them as they relate to curriculum content and current events, and make them integral to the school's daily operations. Exemplary social studies programmes also prepare students to connect knowledge with beliefs and action using thinking skills that lead to rational behaviour in social settings. These include the thinking skills involved in:

(1) acquiring, organising, interpreting, and communicating information;

(2) processing data in order to investigate questions, develop knowledge, and draw conclusions;

(3) generating and assessing alternative approaches to problems and making decisions that are both well informed and justified according to democratic principles; and

(4) interacting with others in empathetic and responsible ways.

Finally, exemplary social studies programmes develop social and civic participation skills that prepare students to work effectively in diverse groups to address problems by discussing alternative strategies, making decisions, and taking action: to pursue social and civic agendas through persuasion, negotiation, and compromise; and to participate actively in civic affairs (e.g., by writing opinion letters to newspapers). Participation in informed public discussion of policy issues is direct preparation for active citizenship, especially when it culminates in decisions and actions that have real consequences. The ideas set forth in the NCSS statement on the "Essentials of the Social Studies" are elaborated in its "Social Studies Curriculum Guidelines".

The guidelines reaffirm that social studies teaching should draw from a broad range of content sources and use varied learning resources and activities. They also emphasise, however, that planning should be guided by basic and long-range social studies goals. Instruction should keep students aware of these goals, and assessments of teaching and learning should focus on the degree to which these goals have been accomplished. Thus, a powerful social studies curriculum is unified by its purposes and goals. All of the components of such a curriculum—not only its content, but its instructional approaches, learning activities, and evaluation methods—are included in the curriculum because they are viewed as means for helping students acquire important capabilities and attitudes.

By itself, the idea of cultural literacy construed in a narrow, name-recognition sense is not considered an adequate basis for content selection. Instead, content is included because it promotes progress toward major social understanding and civic efficacy goals, and it is taught accordingly. That is, instructional methods and activities should be planned to encourage students to connect what they are learning to their prior knowledge and experience, to think critically and creatively about what they are learning, and to use it in authentic application situations.

Learning activities should be introduced and developed so as to make them minds-on activities that engage students with important ideas, not just hands-on activities that may or may not have educational value. In general terms, public commitment, ideal learning conditions, and excellent instruction are equally important and must receive equal attention in educational settings. To provide a social studies programme of excellence, the ingredient that is most often ignored, yet upon which all others depend, is public commitment. Public commitment requires that the public receive information that clearly demonstrates the importance of social studies programmes for the education of all children.

Public commitment also requires that the public recognise all that it takes to support excellence in social studies programmes. It take many things. But when asked to name their most critical need in implementing these standards, teachers, without exception, listed "time." Adequate facilities to foster active learning and house the multitude of materials required to maintain a high-interest laboratory setting are also frequently named by teachers, as are high-quality technology, resources, and opportunities for students to engage in meaningful learning. All of this requires more adequate funding for social studies programmes.

PRINCIPLES OF TEACHING AND LEARNING

The principles are:

1. *Social studies teaching and learning are powerful when they are meaningful:* Students learn connected networks of knowledge, skills, beliefs, and attitudes that they will find useful both in and outside of school. Instruction emphasises depth of development of important ideas within appropriate breadth of topic coverage and focuses on teaching these important ideas for understanding, appreciation, and life application. The significance and meaningfulness of the content is emphasised both in how it is presented to students and how it is developed through activities. Classroom interaction focuses on sustained examination of a few important topics rather than superficial coverage of many. Meaningful learning activities and assessment strategies focus students' attention on the most important ideas embedded in what they are learning. The teacher is reflective in planning, implementing, and assessing instruction.

2. *Social studies teaching and learning are powerful when they are integrative.*

   - Social studies is integrative in its treatment of topics.
   - It is integrative across time and space. Social studies teaching integrates knowledge, skills, beliefs, values, and attitudes to action.

- Social studies teaching and learning integrate effective use of technology.
- Social studies teaching and learning integrate across the curriculum.

3. *Social studies teaching and learning are powerful when they are value-based:* Powerful social studies teaching considers the ethical dimensions of topics and addresses controversial issues, providing an arena for reflective development of concern for the common good and application of social values. Students are made aware of potential social policy implications and taught to think critically and make value-based decisions about related social issues. Rather than promulgating personal, sectarian, or political views, these teachers make sure that students:

   - become aware of the values, complexities, and dilemmas involved in an issue;
   - consider the costs and benefits to various groups that are embedded in potential courses of action; and
   - develop well-reasoned positions consistent with basic democratic social and political values.

   Powerful social studies teaching encourages recognition of opposing points of view, respect for well-supported positions, sensitivity to cultural similarities and differences, and a commitment to social responsibility.

4. *Social studies teaching and learning are powerful when they are challenging:* Students are expected to strive to accomplish the instructional goals, both as individuals and as group members. Teachers model seriousness of

purpose and a thoughtful approach to inquiry and use instructional strategies designed to elicit and support similar qualities from students. Teachers show interest in and respect for students' thinking, but demand well-reasoned arguments rather than opinions voiced without adequate thought or commitment.

5. *Social studies teaching and learning are powerful when they are active:* Active social studies teaching requires reflective thinking and decisionmaking as events unfold during instruction. Students develop new understanding through a process of active construction of knowledge. Interactive discourse facilitates the construction of meaning required to develop important social understanding. Teachers gradually move from providing considerable guidance by modelling, explaining, or supplying information that builds student knowledge, to a less directive role that encourages students to become independent and selfregulated learners. Powerful social studies teaching emphasises authentic activities that call for real-life applications using the skills and content of the field. The teaching and learning document goes on to delineate additional requirements to support an excellent social studies programme which lie beyond the control of the individual teacher. These include:

   - continuous programme assessment; preparation of pre-service teachers that is aligned with curriculum and teaching and learning standards; provision of in-service training to support teachers in understanding and implementing standards;
   - community and governmental support to
   - recognise the subject's vital purpose for civic education

- sustain teacher education and professional development provide adequate funding and leadership.

Successful schools are unique places, not simply spaces. When students conceive of a school as space, they focus on "getting through it" as quickly as possible. Time and destination are foremost in their minds. Rather than having learning as the main focus, their objective is to move on, to get through. Society often reinforces this concept of school by using extrinsic motivational cliches like "finish school to earn more money." Extrinsic motivation with its emphasis on time and destination tends to corrupt true learning. Only rarely do we hear, "Stay in school and learn for your sake as a learner."

Responsibility as educators is to imagine and create places of learning. Such places foster aesthetics, civility, ethics, openness, conversation, security, stewardship/public responsibility, craftsmanship, and individual liberty. Although all educators must take responsibility for creating a learning place, social studies educators should be leaders in this effort. Unless this concept of school is taken seriously, with all the necessary resource and time dimensions, curriculum and instruction will remain a symbolic adventure in rhetoric and retribution. Learning is a dependent variable, relying heavily upon a deep sense of place and community within that place.

A focus on school as a learning place will help students stop simply moving "through" school and instead find the satisfaction that comes from creating and working within a place that values learning. This focus on school as a place for the community of learners will in the end be advantageous to individuals as well as to society as a whole. The elements of curriculum; public commitment, time, and resources; powerful teaching and learning; and the concept of school as a learning place are all essential if students are to achieve the social studies standards we advocate.

Several basic assumptions about the nature of social studies and its place in the school curriculum undergird the vision of powerful social studies presented in this position statement. These fundamental beliefs about social studies are assumed here as given.

1. *Social studies is diverse.* Social studies encompasses many more potential goals and content clusters than can be addressed adequately. Among both social studies teachers and the general public, there is disagreement about the relative importance of major social studies goals and content strands. Consequently, there never has been, and may never be, agreement on a single scope and sequence as the basis for a national social studies curriculum. Recognising this, the NCSS curriculum guidelines state that goal setting and programme development should be undertaken locally in response to locally perceived needs. To inform this process, NCSS has adopted a set of criteria for assessing scope-and-sequence plans and has endorsed three plans that meet these criteria as suitable for use as models by educational agencies and school districts. Locally developed curricula should reflect the essentials of the social studies and embody the principles in the NCSS curriculum guidelines, but their emphasis on goals and content strands can and should vary.

   The same assumption applies to the principles of powerful social studies teaching described here. This position statement does not attempt to prescribe ways to teach particular content because methods must be tailored to local needs. The statement does assume, however, that both the content and the methods of instruction should be selected as means to accomplish major social understanding and civic efficacy goals.

2. All students should have access to the full richness of the social studies curriculum. A complete core curriculum should be available to all students, not just gifted students in advanced programmes. Tracking arrangements should not restrict important learning opportunities. In addition to acquiring basic knowledge and skills, all students at all grade levels should experience a social studies curriculum that includes ongoing engagement in thinking about social and civic problems and policy issues. This includes students at risk of school failure, students whose interests lie in other subject areas or vocational fields, and students who do not plan to attend college.

   Special education students are often mainstreamed into social studies classes. This is as it should be, because all students need exposure to a diverse range of peers and opportunities to address social problems in group settings. Curricular planning for any special education students who are not mainstreamed should include full attention to social studies as well as to other subjects.

3. Teachers need adequate time and resources to teach social studies well at every grade level. The unique social understanding and civic efficacy goals of social studies will not be accomplished if it is treated as a collection of disconnected content to be covered as time allows. Social studies must be viewed as a basic K–12 curriculum component, and teachers and students must be supplied with materials and resources that reflect the students' needs and interests.

4. Social studies teachers need to treat the social world realistically and address its controversial aspects. To accomplish the major goals of this issue-oriented subject, teachers need both the freedom and the fortitude to address the real social world (not simply an idealised version) and to engage students in critical thinking about controversial topics. As they work to help students come to grips with social issues, teachers have both a responsibility to avoid inappropriate promotion of their personal views and a right to expect administrative and community support for their citizen education efforts.

Features of Social Studies Teaching and Learning

Informed by the major purposes and goals of social studies, the assumptions stated above, and the available research and scholarship, this position statement identifies key features of ideal social studies teaching and learning. These features are summed up in the statement that social studies teaching and learning are powerful when they are meaningful, integrative, value-based, challenging, and active. These five key features are considered equally important. They are addressed in the order presented here because such an order creates a natural flow of ideas, not because some key features are considered more essential than others.

Social Studies Teaching and Learning are Powerful when they are Meaningful

Powerful social studies teaching and learning are meaningful to both teachers and students. The content selected for emphasis is worth learning because it promotes progress toward important social understanding and civic efficacy goals, and teaching methods are designed to enable students to appreciate how the content relates to those goals. Rather than memorising disconnected bits of information or practicing skills in isolation, students learn connected networks of knowledge, skills, beliefs, and attitudes that they will find useful both in and outside of school. This worthwhile content is taught in ways that relate to each student's culture and assists the student in recognising its value.

As a result, students' learning efforts are motivated by appreciation and interest, not just by accountability and grading systems. Students become disposed to care about what is happening in the world around them and to use the thinking frameworks and research skills of social science professionals to gather and interpret information. As a result, social learning becomes a lifelong interest and a basis for informed social action. Thoughtfully planned to accomplish significant goals, meaningful social studies teaching embodies several other key features. Instruction emphasises depth of development of important ideas within appropriate breadth of topic coverage and focuses on teaching these important ideas for understanding, appreciation, and life application.

A great many facts, definitions, and generalisations are taught because understanding often-used information and ideas enhances communication within and between cultures. The most effective teachers, however, do not diffuse their efforts by covering too many topics superficially. Instead, they select for emphasis the most useful landmark locations, the most representative case studies, the most inspiring models, the truly precedent-setting events, and the concepts and principles that their students must know and be able to apply in their lives outside of school. Furthermore, teachers inform students of when and how this content will be useful to them in realistic contexts, and they follow through with activities that engage students in applying the content in simulated or real situations.

Facts and ideas are not taught in isolation from other content, nor are skills. Instead, they are embedded in networks of knowledge, skills, beliefs, and attitudes that are structured around important ideas and taught emphasising their connections and potential applications. The significance and meaningfulness of the content is emphasised both in how it is presented to students and how it is developed through activities. New topics are framed with reference to where they fit within the big picture, and students are alerted to their citizen education implications. The new content is developed in ways that help students see how its elements relate to one another (e.g., using diagrams of concept networks or causal chains, lists of key steps in narrative sequences, or other graphic learning aids or illustrations).

Students are encouraged to process what they learn on several levels simultaneously, rather than always starting with low-level factual information and only later engaging in higher-order thinking. From the very beginning, students may be asked to relate new learning to prior knowledge, to think critically about it, or to use it to construct arguments or make informed decisions. Teachers' questions are designed to promote understanding of important ideas and to stimulate thinking about their potential implications. As a result, classroom interaction focuses on sustained examination of a few important topics rather than superficial coverage of many.

Teacher-student interactions emphasise thoughtful discussion of connected major themes, not rapid-fire recitation of miscellaneous bits of information. Meaningful learning activities and assessment strategies focus students' attention on the most important ideas embedded in what they are learning. They encourage students to connect these ideas to their previous knowledge and experience, to think critically and creatively about them, and to consider their social implications. Thus, meaningful social studies teaching emphasises authentic activities and assessment tasks—opportunities for students to engage in the sorts of applications of content that justify the inclusion of that content in the curriculum in the first place.

For example, instead of labelling a map, students might plan a travel route and sketch landscapes that a traveller might see on the route. Instead of listing the amendments in the Bill of Rights, students might discuss or write about the implications of the Bill of Rights for a defendant in a selection of court cases. Instead of filling in a blank to complete the definition of a principle, students might use the principle to make predictions about a related situation or to guide their strategies in a simulation game. This vision of meaningful social studies teaching and learning implies that the teacher is reflective in planning, implementing, and assessing instruction.

Reflective teachers are well informed about the nature and purposes of social studies, and they remain current with developments in the field. They construct well-articulated ideas about their students' citizen education needs, plan their social studies teaching accordingly, and continue to adjust their practices in response to classroom feedback and growth in their own professional knowledge. They work within state and district guidelines, but adapt and supplement these guidelines and their adopted curriculum materials in ways that support their students' social studies education.

In particular, reflective teachers select and present content to students in ways that connect it with the students' interests and with local history, cultures, and issues. Local history and geography receive special attention, as do local examples of social, economic, political, or cultural topics studied at each grade level. There exists a systematic effort to increase awareness and validate the diversity found in the community by involving family members or local ethnic or cultural groups, encouraging students to share their cultural knowledge and experiences, and involving students in the community.

Social Studies Teaching and Learning are Powerful when they are Integrative

Social studies is naturally integrative because it addresses a broad range of content using varied instructional resources and learning activities. But powerful social studies is both integrated and integrative in other respects as well. First, powerful social studies teaching is integrative in its treatment of topics. It crosses disciplinary boundaries to address topics in ways that promote students' social understanding and civic efficacy. Its content is anchored by themes, generalisations, and concepts drawn from the social studies foundational disciplines, supplemented by ideas drawn from the arts, sciences, and humanities, from current events, and from local examples and students' experiences.

Powerfully integrated social studies teaching builds a working knowledge of the evolution of the human condition through time, its current variations across locations and cultures, and an appreciation of the potential implications of this knowledge for social and civic decision-making. Powerful social studies teaching is integrative across time and space, connecting with past experiences and looking ahead to the future. It helps students appreciate how aspects of the social world function, not only in their local community and in the contemporary United States but also in the past and in other cultures.

It puts what is familiar to students into historical, geographical, and cultural perspectives, thus expanding their limited purviews on social phenomena that they may have taken for granted. Powerful social studies teaching integrates knowledge, skills, beliefs, values, and attitudes to action. In particular, it teaches skills within the context of applying knowledge. Skills are included when they are necessary for applying content in natural ways. They are taught directly when opportunities for practice are embedded in authentic application activities. Content flow is not interrupted for practice of related skills. Integrated social studies teaching and learning include effective use of technology that can add important dimensions to students' learning.

Teachers can provide students with information through films, videotapes, videodiscs, and other electronic media, and they can teach students to use computers to compose, edit, and illustrate social studies research reports. Computer-based learning, especially games and simulations, can allow students to apply important ideas in authentic problem-tackling or decision-making contexts. If students have access to computerised data bases, they can search these resources for relevant research information. If they can communicate with peers in other states or nations, they can engage in personalised cultural exchanges or compare parallel data collected in geographically or culturally diverse locations.

Finally, powerful social studies teaching integrates across the curriculum. It provides opportunities for students to read and study text materials, appreciate art and literature, communicate orally and in writing, observe and take measurements, develop and display data, and in various other ways to conduct inquiry and synthesise findings using knowledge and skills taught in all school subjects. Because it addresses such a broad range of content and does so in an integrative fashion that includes attention to ethical and social policy implications, social studies is a natural bridging subject across the curriculum.

Particularly in elementary and middle schools, instruction can feature social studies as the core around which the rest of the curriculum is built. These integrative aspects have the potential for enhancing the scope and power of social studies. They also, however, have the potential for undermining its coherence and thrust as a curriculum component that addresses unique citizen education goals. A literary selection, writing assignment, cooperative learning activity, or computerised simulation cannot be considered curriculum simply because it features social studies combined with some other subject or set of skills. Nor can such activities be substituted for genuine social studies activities.

To qualify as worthwhile elements of social studies curricula, activities must engage students in using important ideas in ways that promote progress toward social understanding and civic efficacy goals. Consequently, programmes that feature a great deal of integration of social studies with other school subjects—even programmes ostensibly built around social studies as the core of the curriculum—do not necessarily create powerful social studies learning. Unless they are developed as plans for accomplishing major social studies goals, such programmes may focus on trivial or disconnected information.

Social Studies Teaching and Learning are Powerful when they are Value-Based

Powerful social studies teaching considers the ethical dimensions of topics and addresses controversial issues providing an arena for reflective development of concern for the common good and application of social values. Students learn to be respectful of the dignity and rights of others when interacting socially, and to emphasise basic democratic concepts and principles when making personal policy decisions or participating in civic affairs. Topics are treated comprehensively and realistically, with attention to their disturbing or controversial aspects.

Students are made aware of potential social policy implications and taught to think critically and make value-based decisions about related social issues. They learn to gather and analyse relevant information, assess the merits of competing arguments, and make reasoned decisions that include consideration of the values within alternative policy recommendations. Through discussions, debates, simulations, research, and other occasions for critical thinking and decision-making, students learn to apply value-based reasoning when addressing social problems. The best social studies teachers develop awareness of their own values and how those values influence their selection of content, materials, questions, activities, and assessment methods. They assess their teaching from multiple perspectives and, where appropriate, adjust it to achieve a better balance.

Rather than promulgating personal, sectarian, or political views, these teachers make sure that students:

(1) become aware of the values, complexities, and dilemmas involved in an issue;

(2) consider the costs and benefits to various groups that are embedded in potential courses of action; and

(3) develop well-reasoned positions consistent with basic democratic social and political values.

The teacher provides guidance to such value-based reasoning especially when it is difficult to discern the connections between core democratic values and the issues at hand, when various core values suggest conflicting policies, or when there is conflict between these core values and students' personal or family values. When this is done most effectively, students may remain unsure about the teacher's personal views on an issue, at least until after it has been discussed thoroughly.

Students become more aware of the complexities involved in addressing the issue in ways that serve the common good, and are more articulate about their own and others' policy recommendations and supporting rationales. Powerful social studies teaching encourages recognition of opposing points of view, respect for well-supported positions, sensitivity to cultural similarities and differences, and a commitment to social responsibility and action. It recognises the reality and persistence of tensions but promotes positive human relationships built on understanding, commitment to the common good, and willingness to compromise and search for common good.

Social Studies Teaching and Learning are Powerful when they are Challenging

Students are expected to strive to accomplish instructional goals both as individuals and as group members through thoughtful participation in lessons and activities and careful work on assignments. To establish a context that will support productively challenging teaching and learning, the teacher encourages the class to function as a learning community. Students learn that the purpose of reflective discussion is to work collaboratively to deepen understanding of the meanings and implications of content. Consequently, they are expected to listen carefully and respond thoughtfully to one another's ideas.

In advancing their own ideas and in responding critically to others, students are expected to build a case based on relevant evidence and arguments and to avoid derisive and other inappropriate behaviour. They are challenged to come to grips with controversial issues, to participate assertively but respectfully in group discussions, and to work productively with partners or groups of peers in cooperative learning activities. Such experiences foster the development of competencies essential to civic efficacy. Making social studies teaching challenging should not be construed as merely articulating high standards and then leaving it to students to try to meet them.

Rather, the teacher models seriousness of purpose and a thoughtful approach to inquiry and uses instructional strategies designed to elicit and support similar qualities from students. The teacher paves the way for successful learning experiences by making sure that the content is suited to the students' developmental levels and cultural backgrounds and by providing assistance that enables students to handle challenging activities. The teacher also makes it clear, however, that students are expected to connect thoughtfully what they are learning to their prior knowledge and experience, to offer comments, and to raise questions. To stimulate and challenge students' thinking, teachers should expose them to many information sources that include varying perspectives on topics and offer conflicting opinions on controversial issues.

Questions call for thoughtful examination of the content, not just retrieval of information from memory. After posing such questions, the teacher allows sufficient time for students to think and formulate responses and to elaborate on their peers' responses. Many of the questions call for critical or creative thinking, suggested solutions to problems, or reasoned positions on policy issues. Such questions often produce numerous and conflicting responses. When this occurs, the teacher withholds evaluation and instead invites the students to engage in sustained dialogue and debate. This shifts some of the authority for evaluating the validity of knowledge from teacher to students. Challenge is also communicated in the teacher's reactions to students' ideas.

The teacher shows interest in and respect for students' thinking, but demands well-reasoned arguments rather than opinions voiced without adequate thought or commitment. Routinely, students are asked to explain and defend their ideas using content-based arguments. Instead of always accepting students' views or asking the class to discuss them, the teacher sometimes challenges students' assumptions or responds with comments or questions that help students identify misconceptions, flaws in the argument, or unrecognised complications.

The teacher must act with sensitivity, because some students become anxious or embarrassed when someone questions their ideas in this way. The teacher makes it clear that the purpose of such a challenge is not to put students on the spot but to help them construct new understanding through engagement in thoughtful dialogue.

Social Studies Teaching and Learning are Powerful when they are Active

Powerful social studies teaching and learning are

rewarding, but they demand a great deal from both teachers and students. Thoughtful preparation and instruction by the teacher and sustained effort by students are required for students to make sense of and apply what they are learning. Powerful social studies teaching demands that the teacher actively make curricular plans and adjustments. Rather than mechanically following the instructions in a manual, an exemplary teacher is prepared to:

(1) acquire and update continuously the subject-matter knowledge and related pedagogical knowledge needed to teach the content effectively;

(2) adjust goals and content to the students' needs;

(3) participate as a partner in learning with students, modelling the joy of both discovering new knowledge and increasing understanding of familiar topics;

(4) use a variety of instructional materials such as physical examples, photographs, maps, illustrations, films, videos, textbooks, literary selections, and computerised databases;

(5) plan field trips, visits to the class by resource people, and other experiences that will help students relate what they are learning to their lives outside the classroom;

(6) plan lessons and activities that introduce content to students, and encourage them to process it actively, think about it critically and creatively, and explore its implications;

(7) develop current or local examples that relate the content to students' lives;

(8) plan sequences of questions that allow for numerous responses and stimulate reflective discussion;

(9) provide students with guidance and assistance as needed, yet encourage them to assume increasing responsibility for managing their own learning;

(10) structure learning environments and activities in ways that encourage students to behave as a community of learners;

(11) use accountability and grading systems that are compatible with instructional methods and that focus on accomplishment of major social understanding and civic efficacy goals; and

(12) monitor reflectively and adjust as necessary.

Besides advance planning and preparation, active social studies teaching requires reflective thinking and decision-making as events unfold during instruction. Teachers must adjust plans to developing circumstances such as teachable moments that arise when students ask questions, make comments, or offer challenges worth pursuing. The teacher decides whether to persist with a topic or conclude it and move on to a new topic, whether to try to elicit an insight from students or to supply it directly, and how thoroughly the students will need to be prepared for an activity before they can begin work on it independently. After the teacher launches an activity and students are working on their own or in collaboration with their peers, the teacher remains active by monitoring individual or group progress and providing assistance.

Interventions are designed to clear up confusion, while enabling students to cope with task demands productively; students should be allowed to handle as much of the task as they can at the moment while at the same time making progress toward fully independent and successful performance. The teacher does not perform the tasks for students or simplify them to the point that they no longer engage the students in the cognitive processes required to accomplish the activity's goals. Students develop new understanding through a process of active construction. They do not passively receive or copy curriculum content; rather, they actively process it by relating it to what they already know (or think they know) about the topic.

Instead of relying on rote learning methods, they strive to make sense of what they are learning by developing a network of connections that link the new content to preexisting knowledge and beliefs anchored in their prior experience. Sometimes the learning involves conceptual change in which students discover that some of their beliefs are inaccurate and need to be modified. The construction of meaning required to develop important social understanding takes time and is facilitated by interactive discourse.

Clear explanation and modelling from the teacher are important, as are opportunities to answer questions about content, discuss or debate the meanings and implications of content, or use the content in activities that call for tackling problems or making decisions. These activities allow students to process content actively and make it their own by paraphrasing it into their own words, exploring its relationship to other knowledge and to past experience, appreciating the insights it provides, or identifying its implications for social or civic decision-making. Teacher and student roles shift as learning progresses.

Early in a unit of study, the teacher may need to provide considerable guidance by modelling, explaining, or supplying information that builds on students' existing knowledge while also assuming much of the responsibility for structuring and managing learning activities. As students develop expertise, however, they can begin to assume responsibility for regulating their learning by asking questions and by working on increasingly complex applications with increasing degrees of autonomy.

The teacher still assists students with challenges they are not yet ready to handle by themselves but such assistance is gradually reduced in response to increases in students' readiness to engage in independent and self-regulating learning. Because what one learns is intimately linked to how one learns it, powerful social studies programmes feature learning that is both social and active. The learning is social because it occurs in a group setting and includes substantial student-student interaction during discussions and collaborative work on activities.

The learning is active because the curriculum emphasises hands-on (and minds-on) activities that call for students to react to what they are learning and use it for some authentic purpose. Effective activities encourage students to think about and apply what they are learning. Teachers may provide opportunities for students to apply their existing knowledge to questions about new content, to understand new content, to synthesise and communicate what they have learned, to generate new knowledge or make creative applications, or to think critically about the content and make decisions or take actions that relate to it.

Powerful social studies teaching emphasises authentic activities that call for using content for accomplishing life applications. For example, critical-thinking attitudes and abilities are developed through policy debates or assignments calling for critique of currently or historically important policy arguments or decisions, not through artificial exercises in identifying logical or rhetorical flaws. Similarly, in addition to more traditional assignments, students frequently engage in cooperative learning, construction of models or plans, dramatic recreations of historical events that shaped democratic values or civic policies, role-play, and simulation activities (e.g., mock trials or simulated legislative activities, interviewing family members, and collecting data in the local community). They also participate in various social and civic roles (e.g., discussing home safety or energy conservation checklists with parents and planning appropriate follow-up action, participating in student government activities and local community restoration or improvement efforts, or doing volunteer work for nursing homes or political campaigns).

Through such activities, students develop social understanding that they can explain in their own words and can access and apply in appropriate situations. For example, they learn to think critically as they read newspapers and magazines, watch television, or monitor political or policy debates. They learn to recognise the problematic aspects of statements, to project the probable social consequences of advocated policies, and to take these complexities into account when forming their opinions. The teacher's modelling, classroom management, motivational techniques, instructional methods, and assessment procedures all communicate to students that they are expected to participate in social studies classes actively and with a sense of purpose.

The students learn to reflect thoughtfully on what they are learning and to ask questions, share opinions, and engage in public content-based dialogue. Through authentic application activities they develop civic efficacy by practicing it—engaging in the inquiry and debate required to make informed decisions about real social issues then following up with appropriate social or civic action.

The kind of powerful social studies teaching and learning envisioned here is realised most fully when it is encouraged and reinforced by other components of the educational system. In particular, powerful social studies teaching and learning are likely to become more common to the extent that:

(1) assessment approaches at all levels focus on measuring progress toward social understanding and efficacy goals;

(2) teachers benefit from effective preservice preparation and in-service professional development programmes, and social studies education receives support from school administrators, parents, the local community, and government agencies; and

(3) the nation successfully meets certain currently recognisable challenges, including the need for additional research on powerful social studies teaching and learning, for improvements in curriculum materials and technologies, and for improvement efforts that focus on accomplishing our most important educational goals.

These systemic influences on social studies education are addressed below.

Assessment Approaches

Powerful social studies teaching and learning include assessment components designed to inform instructional planning and thus produce continuing improvements through successive cycles. The assessment mechanisms focus on the degree to which major social understanding and civic efficacy goals are accomplished, rather than on measuring acquisition of miscellaneous information or command of generic skills. Care is taken to see that testing does not place inappropriate content coverage pressures on teachers or cause them to shift their emphasis away from pursuing major social studies goals.

The NCSS curriculum guidelines call for systematic and rigorous assessment of social studies instruction that is based primarily on each school's stated objectives as the criteria for effectiveness. Knowledge, thinking skills, valuing, and social participation are assessed, using data from many sources in addition to paper-and-pencil tests. These data provide a basis for planning curriculum improvements as well as for assessing students' learning. The guidelines emphasise locally planned assessment of progress toward locally established goals.

In 1991, NCSS elaborated on these guidelines through a position statement on testing and evaluation of social studies students. This statement calls for transforming student assessment from an overreliance on machine-scored standardised tests to approaches that balance such measures with more authentic performance assessments. These include tasks such as speaking effectively or articulating a reasoned stance on a controversial social issue. Such assessments focus on the processes that students use, not merely on the answers they choose. A comprehensive assessment plan for social studies includes daily monitoring of the general effectiveness and quality of student participation in lessons and activities, as well as appropriate use of both criterion- and norm-referenced tests.

The primary purpose of testing should be to improve teaching and learning. To accomplish this purpose, teachers need the freedom and encouragement to select or develop assessment tasks that are suited to their students and aligned with locally adopted social studies goals. This process will involve augmenting traditional tests with performance evaluations, portfolios of student papers and projects, and essays focusing on higher-order thinking and applications. The assessment devices must be fair to all students and interpreted with sensitivity to the propriety of any norms or comparison groups that might be used to place the scores of local students into context.

Teachers must have access to all data collected in their classrooms and be proficient in interpreting and reporting results. A basic underlying principle is that assessment should be aligned with, and designed to help accomplish, the citizen education goals that drive the social studies curriculum. The curriculum's assessment component should not drive its content and process components; instead, all three components should constitute a coherent plan for accomplishing the curriculum's major social understanding and civic efficacy goals.

To the extent that the assessment component creates content or skills coverage pressures that do not promote significant progress toward these goals, it is counterproductive to the purposes of social studies. The same may be true of test-driven coverage pressures in other subject areas if these pressures result in inadequate time allocations to social studies or loss of its coherence as an integral curriculum component.

Support for Powerful Social Studies Teaching

If social studies teaching and learning are to begin to approximate the vision outlined here, more support for social studies education at every level is necessary. Such support includes internal support from the profession itself (emphasising improvements in preservice and in-service teacher education) and external support from parents, the local community, and government agencies.

Preservice teacher preparation

In 1987, NCSS developed a position statement and guidelines on the preparation of social studies teachers. The guidelines refer to admission and continuation of students in teacher education programmes, characteristics of these programmes, and characteristics of the sponsoring institutions. Social studies professionals should lobby for state staffing policies that reflect the NCSS teacher preparation standards. Academic and continuation requirements should ensure that candidates possess sufficient knowledge and skills, as well as appropriate personal and ethical qualities. Programmes should include:

(1) general education preparation in the humanities, the social and behavioural sciences, the natural sciences, mathematics, and computer science;

(2) special emphasis on foundational disciplines for the social studies, approached within a global perspective and with attention to value conflicts and policy issues; and

(3) a professional education component that includes courses in social and philosophical foundations, human growth and development, psychology of learning, needs of exceptional students, gender and ethnic perspectives, use of media, and a range of planning, teaching, and assessment skills.

Social studies methods courses should prepare prospective teachers to select, integrate, and translate knowledge and methodology from the social studies into curricula suitable for the grade levels at which they expect to teach. Programmes should include both information and clinical experiences designed to prepare prospective teachers to teach social studies in a variety of settings to a variety of students using a variety of approaches to curriculum, instruction, and assessment.

Student teaching experiences should span complete school semesters, not just college quarters, and they should be supervised by appropriately qualified cooperating teachers and college or university personnel. Institutions sponsoring teacher education programmes should vest responsibility for managing those programmes in the head of the college, school, or department of education and should staff the programme with faculty members who have experience in K12 schools. These faculty members should excel as teachers or field supervisors, not just as scholars. They should observe and interact with their student teachers in school settings often enough to assess the student teachers' progress accurately and to model or suggest improvements adapted to the settings.

Effective preparation of social studies teachers requires close cooperation between the social science specialists and the teacher education specialists, as well as between the university personnel and school personnel involved in clinical and field experiences. All of the participants in teacher education programmes should understand and be committed to major social studies goals, should be knowledgeable about powerful social studies teaching, and should model such teaching in their classrooms. This implies use of a broad range of teaching and learning methods.

Prospective teachers need coaching and structured opportunities to develop their skills at using approaches such as lecture and discussion, cooperative learning, panel discussions, debates, games, simulations, community participation expericnces, and computerised data bases and learning programmes. Besides learning the procedural aspects of these varied approaches, prospective teachers should learn to shift their managerial and instructional roles appropriately and to prepare students to assume additional responsibilities for managing their learning.

Teachers need to function comfortably not just as experts but also as guides. Learning to plan, implement, and assess powerful social studies teaching on a consistent basis will require years of guided in-service and self-assessment experiences in addition to good preservice preparation. At a minimum, however, preservice programmes should equip new teachers with a basic understanding of social studies purposes and goals and a vision of powerful social studies teaching and learning that they can use to guide their subsequent professional development.

Supporting in-service Teachers

The vision of powerful social studies teaching and learning outlined here assumes local planning and decision-making in which teams of teachers identify and clarify goals, plan the social studies programme, monitor it reflectively, and make necessary adjustments. To make this possible, school districts and building administrators need to allocate sufficient in-class time for social studies teaching and provide sufficient out-of-class time for collegial planning and professional development.

Although social studies is rich in opportunities for connecting content from other subjects, it features important purposes and goals of its own and must be taught with frequency and coherence for these goals to be accomplished. Throughout grades K–12, all students should receive daily instruction in a carefully planned social studies programme. Teaching staffs need collegial planning time and in-service staff development activities to ensure that all teachers develop a shared understanding of the broad goals of social studies education and thus approach them with an emphasis on building social understanding and civic efficacy. Guided by these major goals and a knowledgeable social studies coordinator, collegial planning should yield a coherent social studies programme for the entire school.

All teachers should know what their colleagues are doing and understand how the components assigned to their grade level fit into the big picture. Planning should be guided by the NCSS collection of curriculum planning resourccs and should incorporate the instructional principles outlined in this position statement. The programme should include an assessment component that aligns with goals and complements the other programme components (the value and attitudinal aspects as well as the knowledge and skills aspects). Teachers need support for acquiring and receiving social studies information, resources, and teaching and assessment strategies.

All teachers need opportunities to obtain information about and assistance in using social studies resources from competent consultants, opportunities to visit other classrooms to see demonstrations of powerful teaching and learning, and involvement in decision-making concerning adoption of curriculum materials or other changes in the school's social studies programme. New teachcrs need mentoring from accomplished teachers. Teachers with special interests or assignments need release time and support for attendance at state and national conferences, activity in professional organisations, local networking, and the opportunity to help develop curriculum materials or programme plans.

Teachers should be encouraged to identify their group and individual professional development needs relating to social studies, and arrangements should be made to address these needs. Experienced teachers interested in doing so may apply for assessment and NCSS advanced professional certification of the quality of their social studies teaching. Whether or not they seek council certification in addition to their state certification, however, teachers who have continuing responsibility for social studies education should strive to meet NCSS's standards for certified professionals. In particular, they should:

(1) continue their professional development through formal course work, attendance at conferences, professional reading, and collaboration with peers on action research or staff development projects;

(2) analyse their and their students' work products;

(3) keep a journal on practice; and

(4) take active roles in professional and community organisations.

Social studies education should receive vigorous support as a vital curriculum component responsible for accomplishing uniquely important purposes and goals. A social studies coordinator should be appointed for the district as a whole and for each building. The district should provide appropriate instructional time, materials and resources, facilities, and equipment for all teachers. They will need access to carefully selected textbooks and the many types of data sources that are used in powerful social studies teaching, including auxiliary texts, multimedia kits, reference materials and text supplements at various reading levels, maps, globes, physical artifacts, films and tapes, computer equipment and software, content-correlated literature selections, and equipment for simulations or special events.

Districts should encourage their social studies teachers to participate in active curriculum committees that have decision-making as well as advisory responsibilities. Finally, a district-wide policy statement on academic freedom and responsibility should be in place. Social studies teachers should be able to rely on this statement and on administrative support for their efforts to model civic participation and assist their students to confront social issues.

Community and Governmental Support

Several forms of community and governmental support will be required to sustain powerful social studies programmes. Most fundamentally, communities and governments need to recognise the subject's vital purpose for citizen education and thus prepare to support accomplishment of its social understanding and civic efficacy goals and the powerful forms of teaching and learning necessary to accomplish them. This commitment implies sustaining teacher education and professional development programmes and forms of support for social studies in schools as described in previous sections.

These aspects of powerful social studies programmes require funding and leadership support from local school districts and state governments. Corporate and business interests can be supportive as well. Sponsoring cooperative programmes, hosting field trips, supplying guest speakers, and supporting local heritage preservations that serve as school resources are just some of the ways local businesses and communities can support their schools' social studies programmes. Parents can help by donating or lending cultural or historical artifacts, acting as chaperones on field trips, and visiting classes or resource people (e.g., to provide information about their occupations or their ethnic heritages).

Future Challenges

The vision of powerful social studies teaching and learning set forth here has been informed by a growing knowledge base about the ingredients for teaching social studies for understanding, appreciation, and life application. This position statement, however, is just a beginning. The future holds many challenges that must be met if the vision of powerful social studies teaching and learning outlined here is to be developed in more detail and become the basis for standard practice in the schools. More research on socal studies teaching and learning is needed, especially research that focuses on teachers' efforts to develop social understanding and civic efficacy in their students.

Studies that document the effects of powerful social studies teaching and describe it in detail as it unfolds across a lesson or curriculum unit would be especially valuable. Also needed are studies of what students at the various grade levels know (or think they know) about the content taught in those grades and how instruction affects their thinking. This information then can be used to develop ways to adapt instruction so as to build on students' valid knowledge and address their misconceptions. As the knowledge base develops, it will need to consider the situational characteristics of various teaching contexts.

The general principle that social studies teaching and learning become more powerful when they are meaningful, integrative, value-based, challenging, and active applies to all social studies classes, but the specifics involved in bringing this principle to life will vary according to individual students and content areas. More information is needed about the particular forms of powerful social studies teaching that best suit various grade levels and content areas, how to adapt these forms of instruction to meet the needs of diverse learners, and what constitutes effective pre-service and in-service social studies teacher education. Improved learning resources, along with research on how to use them effectively, are also needed.

Textbooks need to be structured coherently around powerful ideas developed in depth, and they need to be supplemented with a wide range of learning resources and activities. In the early elementary grades, multimedia kits, picture books, simplified maps, collections of artifacts (or realistic reproductions), and other instructional tools and data sources designed for students who have not yet become sophisticated readers are needed. Across the grades, computerised data bases, simulations, and games, laserdiscs, hypermedia, scanners, electronic mail connections with classrooms in other states or nations, and production and use of videotapes as teaching and learning devices have potential for social studies applications.

These applications will need to be developed and studied to determine how to make the best use of their unique capabilities in the most cost-effective ways. Research and development also need to attend to the changes in the teacher's role entailed in many of these innovations. Along with access to new resources and technologies, teachers will need guidance on how to manage these multiple resources and help their students learn to use them more effectively. Certain systematic changes in education in the United States are needed to support fully powerful social studies teaching and learning. Most of these are changes that would improve the quality of instruction across the curriculum.

5

Qualitative Teaching

Teachers do not enter the classroom as finished products. Most teachers who remain in the profession improve and grow over time and become better. Good teachers produce good students. A teacher's most important task is contributing to and enhancing the learning and achievement of his or her students. While there is some evidence about the qualifications of those who enter the profession, there is a need for more information and research on the quality of teachers' classroom practices, on the impact of those practices over time, and on how professional development programmes support improved teaching and learning.

What are the characteristics of teachers who consistently improve the achievement of their students? A large segment of the education research community is engaged in attempting to answer this challenging question. Promising progress is now being made in creating data systems to identify the attributes and strategies of teachers whose students, over periods of several years, have achieved unusually large gains in the subjects taught.

There are certain things we know about teacher quality. A correlation exists between a teacher's verbal ability and student achievement. Teachers who have majored in the subject they teach are better teachers of that subject than those who have not. Pedagogy, particularly content-based pedagogy, has a positive impact on student achievement, and teachers with considerable experience are likely to make a greater contribution to student learning than teachers with few years of teaching experience.

Knowing Content

To be highly qualified, teachers must meet three general requirements: have a bachelor's degree, be licensed or certified by the state, and demonstrate subject matter competence in each academic subject they teach. The definition of teacher quality differs depending on the level of students being taught and whether a teacher is new or already teaching. New elementary teachers must demonstrate their knowledge and teaching skills by passing a rigorous state test in reading, writing, math, and other areas of the elementary curriculum. New middle/secondary teachers may demonstrate competency in each academic subject they will teach by having a major or equivalent coursework, a graduate degree, or an advanced credential—or, alternatively, by passing a rigorous state academic subject test—in each subject to be taught.

Veteran teachers with three or more years' experience should have an opportunity to demonstrate that they have achieved a high level of proficiency in their content area and also in the skills and art of actual classroom practice. States could:

- raise the bar for content rigor by reviewing and increasing passing scores on teacher licensure content examinations.

- grant a content "pass" to all veteran teachers who reached the new passing score when initially assessed.
- institute an ongoing series of rigorous, uniform performance assessments, to be administered to veteran teachers by trained reviewers following a standard observation protocol.
- utilise teacher performance assessment data in concert with student achievement data as indicators of teacher quality.

Knowing one's subject, knowing how to teach it, and actually being able to teach it are all critical. Excellent teaching combines passion and art along with academic prowess. There is some evidence that the public holds this view as well. In *Quality, Affordability, and Access: Americans Speak on Higher Education*, a public opinion poll conducted by Democratic pollster Peter Hart and Republican pollster Robert Teeter, one-third or more of the public cites having the skills to design inspiring learning experiences and having a caring attitude toward students as the two most important qualities for a good K-12 teacher.

Competent, skilled teachers should possess the following four types of knowledge and skills:

- basic academic reading, writing, and math
- thorough knowledge of the content of each subject taught, appropriate to the levels of their students
- both generic and content-specific knowledge in areas such as child development, classroom management, motivating children to learn, interpreting and using assessment data, individualising instruction, aligning content to the state's standards, developing appropriate instructional materials, and working with children with disabilities or from other cultures'

- actual hands-on ability and skill to use the above types of knowledge to engage students successfully in learning and mastery

Teaching Progression

Novices can develop and mature into excellent teachers. It is erroneous to assume that once in the classroom, the teacher is a finished product. When they first enter the classroom, new teachers do not possess all the knowledge and skills they will need to become highly effective. With experience, practice, assistance and training, however, novices can learn and improve to become better teachers.

There is another type of teachers called exemplary teachers. This is not a beginning teacher, but an experienced teacher that the law describes as one who meets the "highly qualified" requirements and is recommended as exemplary by administrators and others; mentors other teachers, helping them improve their instructional strategies and skills; develops curricula; and offers other forms of professional development. This is the ultimate, highest quality teacher that the nation seeks for every classroom.

The profession of teaching is a continuum, from pre-service preparation to initial licensure, to hiring and induction, continued practice and professional development through mastery and advanced certification. The graphic below offers a time-line perspective illustrating the transitions in the developing career of a teacher. Particularly striking is the brief period from preparation (teacher education) to hiring (licensure), and the lengthy expanse of on-the-job classroom teaching (professional development and teacher performance evaluation). The pre-employment phase consumes only about one-tenth of a full 40-year, lifetime teaching career. It is during the time spent teaching in the classroom that teachers, given proper support, evaluation, feedback, and targeted professional development, can evolve and mature into accomplished, exemplary teachers.

A critical factor in this developmental progress is the alignment of the state student content standards throughout the continuum. This is essential for both equity and efficacy in helping students meet the standards on which they will be tested—and on which, increasingly in the future, teachers' performance will be based. Alignment of state standards should be evidenced in pre-service preparation, licensure exams, curricula, related professional development efforts, and teacher performance evaluations. Just as students must be exposed to curricula linked to the standards upon which they are assessed, teachers must be prepared to teach such curricula before their effectiveness is evaluated.

Teacher Preparation

In America, Title of the Higher Education Act, currently being reauthorised by the US Congress, includes accountability provisions for the nation's teacher education programmes. A key requirement is the annual reporting of the pass rates of each institution's graduates on state teacher licensure exams. Pass rate data are important but that additional information is needed, including data on candidates' actual scaled scores, to provide more useful information about the quality of preparation programmes. Yes/No pass rate data do not indicate the range or the distribution of candidate scores, providing information of limited use as a result. Further, the fact that different states set different passing scores on the same licensing tests makes cross-state comparisons impossible. Thus, using pass rate data in concert with scaled scores and other output measures about the programme may provide reason to remediate or celebrate.

Even with additional output measures, we need to understand something about the candidate pool. Teacher candidates vary according to their literacy skills, content knowledge and motivation to succeed—qualities that are not equally distributed among candidates at various institutions. Thus, it is difficult to ascertain whether high test scores are due to significant student growth resulting from an institution's rigorous preparation programme or to the pre-existing skills and drive of those students who chose to attend it.

Teacher Licensure

Licensure is an important element to assure quality in the teaching workforce of each state. The purpose of teacher licensure, however, is often misunderstood. Licensure is used to identify those teacher candidates with the knowledge and skills deemed important for a beginning practitioner. Initial licensure represents a beginning for the novice. The newly certified candidate has earned the right of passage to a profession that, like others, is characterised by an upward progression of knowledge and skill, achieved over time through additional learning, practice, experience, and maturity. Licensure establishes a floor; it does not ensure excellent practice. That determination can only occur in the context of teaching.

Typically, states offer an initial provisional license at the time of hiring. After serving successfully for several years on the job, the teacher may then apply for a permanent license, which is subject to renewal after a set period of time.

Whatever the route, responsible licensing decisions include three key components:

– education

– experience

– examination

The rôle of the teacher in advancing learning is so important that education, an examination, or experience alone will not provide a sufficient basis to make an appropriate decision regarding licensure. All three are critically important.

Tests are usually one of several criteria necessary for licensure. Licensure tests by their very nature are intended to distinguish between those who have the desired level of competence to begin practice from those who do not. The tests are measures of knowledge—knowledge of basic academic skills, of subject matter, and of how to teach. They do not, however, measure one's competence in the classroom, nor do they indicate how well a teacher communicates with students or engages students' interest in learning.

Historically, licensure tests have not been designed to predict performance. For example, the bar examination does not predict how good a lawyer someone will be or the number of cases that person may win. Similarly, teacher licensure tests have traditionally not been held to the standard of predicting outcomes—but the changing environment in school accountability has produced increased interest in holding them to this higher standard.

The concept of alternative routes to teaching, including reducing unnecessary barriers and expediting the process to encourage the entry of new, talented candidates into the field is higly appreciable. While the relative weight assigned to each of the three factors noted above (Education, Experience and Examination) may change in order to open the door to prospective teachers, regardless of what route a teacher follows, all three components are needed. We believe that states should prescribe a consistent and uniform licensure standard for all candidates—a standard that aligns to the state's student content standards and to the knowledge and skill requirements the state has defined for teaching various subject areas and grade levels. We encourage the development of public policies that require graduates of alternative programmes to face the same accountability requirements of their traditionally prepared peers.

Licensure offers great potential to enhance the quality of teaching across the country. Because state practices and policies vary considerably, a uniform national standard does not exist. States should re-evaluate their existing teacher licensure programmes and begin work on raising the standards for those entering the profession. Specifically, states should agree on a common national standard for subject-area tests and set cutoff scores at a level that requires teaching candidates to demonstrate mastery reflecting at least two years of undergraduate study.

Induction and Mentoring

It is essential for all states to establish induction programmes for beginning teachers that provide teachers with mentoring and other support during the crucial first years of teaching. Research shows that teachers without induction support leave the profession at rates almost 70 percent higher than those who receive it. With about one-third of new teachers leaving the classroom within three years and nearly one-half within five years, not providing induction is an irresponsible decision. In some countries both require and finance mentoring programs for all novice teachers—a dismal record, especially since significant federal funds are available for this purpose. Others have echoed this conclusion, recommending a mentor for all new teachers throughout their first year.

A recent study commissioned by the California Commission on Teacher Credentialing examined the impact of the Beginning Teacher Support and Assessment/CFASST on the teaching effectiveness of beginning teachers and on the learning of the students of these teachers. Overall, the findings showed a positive impact of BTSA/CFASST on teachers and students and confirmed the model of how BTSA/CFASST works: the support of an experienced teacher, the curriculum of CFASST events, and the improved practices, in turn, lead to improved student learning. Essential to good mentoring programmes is a cadre of highly skilled mentors who are able to quickly diagnose the needs of struggling teachers and can constructively relate to and support them.

Continuous Professional Development

Continuous professional development is critical to developing and maintaining high quality teachers. Without highly skilled support, even those with high qualifications will not remain in the profession long enough to make a difference in children's lives. The Teaching Commission urges principals to ensure that all teachers have the chance to improve their classroom instruction by receiving ongoing training aimed at professional growth and better student outcomes. Principals should be held responsible for ensuring that all teachers benefit from scientifically based professional development opportunities that focus squarely on assessing and improving instructional practices and thereby raising student achievement. The development of each of the products for professional development, designed to improve teacher and school leader performance, are grounded in what research studies define as best practice

Performance Evaluation

Evaluations of teachers' performance in the classroom occur at many points on the teaching continuum, at various times throughout a school year, and for a variety of purposes. These can include relatively low-stakes evaluations, such as ones that provide remediation to a teacher candidate, determine assistance required by a novice in the induction/ mentoring period, or identify the effects of a professional development programme, or evaluations for more high-stakes decisions, such as licensure, hiring, performance pay, promotion, or tenure.

The teaching skills and content knowledge of teachers should be routinely observed in the classroom and evaluated throughout their careers. Unfortunately, performance evaluation is frequently a missing element of teacher development planning and, as noted earlier, when used to assist fledgling candidates, can mean the difference between leaving and staying.

Strong content knowledge and knowing how to teach are both essential qualifications that beginning teachers must have to enter the classroom. Teachers who meet high qualifications for entering the profession can grow and improve their practice as they progress in the profession. States should work together to achieve more commonality and comparability in qualifications for those entering and staying in this important profession. More specifically, public policy-makers to adopt policies on three critical issues highlighted below:

- Defining teacher quality:
  - Good teachers produce good students. That is the primary purpose of teaching and the basis upon which teachers should be evaluated.
  - Good teaching requires four types of knowledge and skills: (1) basic academic skills, (2) thorough content knowledge of each subject to be taught, (3) knowledge of both generic and content-specific pedagogy, and (4) hands-on teaching skills.
- Raising standards for entry:
  - States should re-evaluate their teacher licensure programmes and begin raising their entry standards, including the passing scores required on licensure exams.
  - inclusion of sustained clinical teaching experience in teacher preparation and as a condition of programme approval and teacher licensure.
  - Teacher candidate pass rate data are not enough; candidates' scaled test scores will provide additional, useful information about the quality of their teacher preparation.
- Supporting teachers:
  - All states should establish induction programmes for beginning teachers, providing mentoring and support during the first years of teaching.

- Continuous high quality professional development is critical to developing and maintaining high quality teachers.
- Greater emphasis should be placed on observing and evaluating teachers' teaching skills and content knowledge in their actual classrooms throughout their careers.

6

Teaching ICTs

In the science and engineering fields, computational technologies are changing the ways in which scientific research is carried out. Modeling and simulation tools, along with wide-scale deployment of grid technologies, allow scientists and engineers to work in ways that were not previously possible. Networking tools facilitate the exchange of ideas and scientific instrumentation and data across time, distance, and disciplines, making distributed-knowledge environments an essential component of research-based enterprises. Innovation is more of a necessity now than ever before. And yet a number of recent reports make it clear that the world is losing ground on key indicators of innovation and progress. Pre-college education, in particular, is lagging well behind its mandate to educate all children to higher standards, especially in areas that prepare students for careers in science, technology, engineering, and mathematics.

Science and engineering enrollments at the college and university levels are showing troubling signs of decline. Universities are facing increasing competition from overseas institutions for the best students, resulting in declining enrollments of foreign students. Enrollments are not expanding to fill the gap; in fact, some science and engineering fields such as computer science have experienced precipitous declines in enrollment.

International indicators of pre-college students' progress paint a more troubling picture. Results from the Third International Mathematics and Science Study (TIMSS) show that mathematics performance among U.S. eighth-grade students is lower than that of fourteen other countries, putting them well behind the highest-performing countries. Clearly, the challenges facing "pre-K to gray" education are of magnitudes that require grand and ambitious strategies, not only to halt the decline in students' progress, but also to reinvigorate the system to lead the world in innovation and excellence.

Historically, the National Science Foundation (NSF) has been at the forefront of supporting research and development efforts that lead to significant advances in science and industry. Its role in supporting innovation in the K-12, undergraduate, and graduate sectors has been equally significant. For instance, The National Science Digital Library (NSDL) was created by NSF to provide organised access to high-quality resources and tools that support innovations in teaching and learning at all levels of STEM education. The library currently contains more than 800,000 STEM educational resources from 500 partner libraries. NSF funding also helped to create Cognitive Tutor Algebra, a full-year algebra course based on cognitive psychology theory and artificial intelligence technology that is associated with increased student achievement and is now in regular use in 2,000 U.S. schools.

Another example of NSF's influence across the STEM curriculum includes the Technology Enhanced Learning in Science (TELS) Center at one of the NSF Centers for Learning and Teaching. TELS is building upon NSF-funded research to support science learning mediated by Web-based technologies, such as modeling and simulation, for all science courses in grades 6-12. The objective of The CELF Initiative to create the Cyberinfrastructure for Education and Learning for the Future is to ensure that "pre-K to gray" learning and teaching are informed by 21st century technological developments, learning sciences, and STEM research.

Learners of all ages would be able to reap the full benefits of the s scientific Cyberinfrastructure by engaging with scientific data sets, instruments, models, and simulations. Moreover, the new educational Cyberinfrastructure will make it possible to collect and analyse data continually from millions of educational activities nationwide over a period of years, enabling new advances in the sciences of learning and providing systematic ways of measuring progress at all levels. However, creating such an infrastructure in a way that meets the needs and respects the rights of all participants in the educational process requires that significant technical challenges be addressed.

Although the envisioned Cyberinfrastructure alone cannot cure the problems of lagging performance and inadequate enrollments in STEM fields, it could have a significant impact if it is properly informed by learning sciences research and linked to educational practice. By transcending the boundaries of formal and informal learning-and by helping students experience what it is like to engage in scientific inquiry, evidence-based argumentation, and engineering practice. Having more quantitative data available on learner performance will make it possible to optimise each learner's educational experience, identifying strengths and needs and providing online or real-time support as it is required. The ability to respond and provide remediation based on individual needs should improve the performance of educational systems at all levels.

More than three decades of investment in multiple pre-college R&D programmes have generated valuable lessons that can be used to inform this next generation of education funding at all levels. These lessons include:

- Instructional approaches based on solid science on how people learn can yield large gains in student learning and engagement.
- The claim that technology holds the promise of radically changing the learning of science, technology, engineering, and mathematics should be pursued with a clear understanding of the impact of the fundamentally cultural, social, and contextual nature of both learning and technology use. Professional training ideally will support teachers to further solidify their own content knowledge and skills, as well as increase their ability to effectively impart this knowledge to their students. The power of new technologies to advance learning will not be fully realised without close attention to the social context in which those technologies are used.
- Teachers need pre-service and in-service professional development on using technology, but most importantly on how best to use it to support the acquisition of domain knowledge and reasoning skills, metacognitive development, and sustained interest and motivation. The need for highly qualified teachers is well documented, and Cyberinfrastructure technologies and methodologies will place new demands on their talents.

- Education and educational technology use must keep up with ever-changing economic, social, and cultural needs.
- Assessment practices must be adapted to these changes and better represent the true needs of society, and not simply pursue an uninvestigated repetition of K-12 formal education. Cyberinfrastructure offers the potential to improve or reinvent assessment practices. Given the strong impact the nature of assessment has on how and what students learn, testing must be adapted to emphasise the opportunities that Cyberinfrastructure offers for allowing students to go beyond knowing science to understanding science.

There are also important concerns for the future:

- As STEM research becomes increasingly collaborative, distributed, and dependent upon access to large amounts of computational power and data, students as well as teachers and educational decision makers at all levels will need to learn how to think with data-using diverse forms of data, information resources, tools, and services in many different fields of study to support making a broad range of decisions. They will need to become proficient in navigating a rich universe of data resources; in engaging with statistics, probability and evidence-based argumentation; and in discerning the authenticity, quality and reputation of these data sources. Emerging tools and frameworks for interactive and dynamic visualisations of patterns in data will be integral to these new literacies for thinking and decision making.
- Today, students do not have equal access to high-quality instructional resources, nor do they have equal access to highly qualified teachers, particularly for

> higher-level science and mathematics courses. With the increasing diversity of native languages in the nation's schools and workplaces, the challenges of meeting multilingual needs are an important aspect of this access problem. Ensuring that materials are designed to address the learning challenges of underserved populations and communities is a national imperative.

In keeping with scientific trends and developments, *Cyberinfrastructure for Education and Learning for the Future,* or *CELF* is an expanded vision of Cyberinfrastructure R&D. CELF will provide learners, educators, and other stakeholders with access to, and the ability to participate in, long-lived, large-scale educational experiences, encompassing real-world experiential learning, simulation, modeling, educational games, automated assistance from virtual peers and intelligent tutors, and Web-based access to authentic learning resources and scientific data. It will include tools that facilitate the creation and adaptation of learning experiences with digital resources, and data collection and analysis tools that make it possible to evaluate a learner's progress on a continual and longitudinal basis. CELF will make possible the compilation, analysis, and distillation of unprecedented amounts of human performance and learning data, with built-in provisions for data protection, privacy, and control. It will provide a foundation for science learning that is computationally enabled and empirically based, coupled with innovations in educational practice.

Consider the following scenario. The context of this particular image is a "serious game," that is, an interactive experience that promotes learning and is entertaining.

Learners cooperate in designing and conducting a mission to Mars, in the context of a game-based simulation.

In the course of the project they carry out a variety of STEM-related learning activities, spanning physics, chemistry, biology, engineering and mathematics. These become springboards for seeking other learning resources outside the game, and collaborating with other learners in online working groups. Learners access online science and engineering data sets and models in order to compare their predictions against results from space scientists. They receive guidance in inquiry skills, metacognitive learning skills, and collaboration skills. The game itself is constructed and adapted through the collaborative efforts of the participating learners. In his earth sciences course, John, for example, studies terrain data from Mars Rover missions and creates a model of the Martian terrain to be explored by others. Manuela, in her high-school engineering class, designs an autonomous rover vehicle to collect geologic samples and constructs a simulation of her rover design for use in the mission. She can then compare her model's performance in the simulation against records of actual Mars Rover missions. Sherry, the teacher, is assisted by virtual assistant teachers (intelligent tutors) embedded in the game that help her monitor learner progress and offer guidance and challenges. One of Sherry's virtual assistants reports that Manuela is having difficulty getting the controller of her virtual robot to work, and is not availing herself of online resources, so Sherry suggests that she discuss her design with an online community of robot enthusiasts. Data collected from learner performance within and surrounding the game provide the teacher with documentation and evidence of learning progress relating to curriculum standards and goals. In some contexts this may replace the need for standardised tests, but in others the teacher already has sufficient evidence to predict that the learners will meet the required standards.

Serious games such as this are becoming increasingly common in public policy, healthcare, and military training, as well as for corporate training and all levels of education. CELF can help turn serious games from narrowly focused experiences created for special purposes to a broad-based, long-lived experience. Such research is inherently multidisciplinary, involving the entire NSF, STEM professionals in partnership with computer and information science and engineering (CISE), social, behavioral and economic (SBE) researchers, and a full range of educational researchers (e.g., learning scientists, sociologists, psychologists and cognitive scientists, and teacher educators).

Furthermore, given the integrated and long-term nature of such an endeavor, every effort must be made to ensure that CELF research is coordinated and inclusive. It is expected that learning and education through CELF should be increasingly personalised, interactive, and tailored to meeting a learner's curricular, motivational, metacognitive and social needs. Personalised learner interactions should be realised not only in formal classes with "conventional" computers, but also in informal educational settings where they are mediated through a range of personal ubiquitous devices. To meet individual needs, assessment will be continuous and dynamic, aimed at monitoring and supporting learners to develop their cognitive and metacognitive skills. Such learning is not the right of a privileged, digitally and educationally sophisticated few, but instead is inclusive and accessible for all.

There are five issues that illustrate the potential of the Cyberinfrastructure for transforming educational practice, given the appropriate conditions, that will need to be addressed.

1. *Blending Formal and Informal Learning*: : How does the Cyberinfrastructure transcend the conventional boundaries of school-based education?
2. *Lifelong Learning Chronicles* : How do we develop a rich qualitative and quantitative record of learning over time in a way that dynamically informs a multitude of stakeholders?
3. *Teaching Through the Cyberinfrastructure* : What are the new images of teaching and teachers afforded by the Cyberinfrastructure?
4. *Communities of Learners* : How can the Cyber-infrastructure support and transform communities of learners?
5. *Educational Policy and the Cyberinfrastructure* : What changes in processes, policies, and support are necessary to achieve those educational experiences?

Blending Formal and Informal Learning

Cyberinfrastructure for Education and Learning for the Future (CELF) will change the way learning takes place both inside and outside the classroom, blurring the distinctions between the two. Technologymediated learning will take place in the context of computationally augmented real-world environments, online communities of practice, interactive virtual environments, games, simulations, models, and audio/ video/IM/SMS communications-not just in classrooms. Learning occurs now in these milieus, but largely independent of one another and uninformed by educational research. It is increasingly apparent that informal and lifelong learning is the key solution to equipping people with the evolving knowledge and skills that will be needed to adapt to the continuously changing nature of society.

Consider the following scenario for its image of blending formal and informal learning:

The classes John and Manuela attend take mobile devices [including a phone, camera, personal digital assistants (PDAs), embedded sensors, location-aware global positioning systems (GPS)] into a local town. They explore the town, learning about its history over the past 100 years and the people who have lived in the town, as well as its physical and political geography. As they reach hotspots they receive specific information, which will be different according to different learner profiles. John's PDA speaks some of this information once it detects that he is having difficulty reading some of the texts and is becoming distressed by his inability to keep up. The students take photographs, record audio messages and video and take sensor readings of temperature, pollution, and humidity. Manuela has a particular interest in geology and is collecting soil samples. When her digital agent tells Manuela that her friend Beth is near the town museum, she asks Beth to check out what's available. The students share the information they are collecting with each other and with other students back in school. The next day, the whole class interacts with these data to collate, represent and analyse them. They compare their data to those collected by students in other schools and in previous years. Manuela sends some of her results of the geological survey back to the museum where it is incorporated into the exhibition. Several weeks later, a proud Manuela takes her parents back to the museum to see the results of her work.

Teachers need to integrate the best aspects of technology-mediated informal learning into classroom learning, making it possible for in-class and out-of-class learning to support each other to a greater extent than they do now. Furthermore, the opportunities for learning are not limited to a classroom, but can occur in any place and at any time. They do not suddenly stop when a school bell rings or the semester ends. To effectively achieve this vision, innovations in the Cyberinfrastructure itself will be needed, as well as coordinated multidisciplinary and interdisciplinary research in how best to exploit the potential of the new Cyberinfrastructure.

Two important areas for CELF-1) portable and personal technologies, and 2) virtual learning environments, including virtual resource centers and digital libraries, games, simulations and modeling-are identified below and characterised in some detail.

Portable and Personal Technologies

Portable and personal technologies are a ubiquitous part of modern life. For example, Prensky estimates that there are 1.5 billion mobile phones in the world, and 80 percent of the world's population lives within range of a cellular network. In some countries, particularly in Europe, mobile penetration is at 100 percent; in the United States, 40 percent of junior high students and 75 percent of high school students have mobile phones. Furthermore, the processing power of top-end mobile phones and PDAs is only a decade behind the computing power of desktop computers. For current and future generations of learners, it is increasingly likely that their main interaction with the digital world will be through such devices. Consequently, one of the main challenges facing educators is to move from the prevailing view of mobile technologies as disruptive devices that have no place in a classroom to understanding how best to exploit the substantial opportunities that such devices offer.

We are only beginning to understand the opportunities that portable and personal technologies-known as "mobiles"-provide for learning. However, they have a number of distinct characteristics. They are lightweight and highly portable, encourage communication and connectivity, enable new forms of collaborative learning, can respond or gather information from the environment in a time- and locationaware manner, and can be personalised to meet different learners' requirements. These characteristics of mobiles support many different innovative learning practices:

- They can be used as classroom response systems to gather student responses, showing anonymised individual views as well as aggregate data.
- They can provide mixed reality tours of museums, galleries, and the wider environment. For example, the Archeoguide project aims to provide an augmented reality reconstruction of the ruins in ancient monuments, which are adapted to the specific interests of each visitor.
- They allow learners to take part in participatory simulations and games. For example, in the Savannah project, school children play the part of lions roaming around their environment (a school playing field) using location-aware PDAs. They learn how to mark their territory (with scents indicated on PDAs), collaborate to hunt large prey (when they reach a hotspot they may be told they are hungry or that there is an elephant nearby), and retreat to a den to reflect on success and failure. By becoming lions, children have many opportunities to understand the reasons for lions' behavior.

- They can support teachers in their professional practice. Perry found the practical features of PDAs-such as sise, synchronisation features and battery life-helped school administrators and teachers coordinate meetings, assess attendance and truancy, and organise lesson plans. Tatar et al. emphasise the importance of teacher involvement in the design of these learning technologies.

- They may be able to reach learners who are disadvantaged by the digital divide: in Europe up to 80 percent of young homeless people have access to mobile phones, and a new family of extremely inexpensive cell phones are already patented and being manufactured. The M-learning project is exploring how mobile phones can improve basic literacy and numeracy skills for disadvantaged young people. Typical applications include the use of phones to provide games, multimedia messaging to add visual and audio material to Web-based graphics, and text messaging to supply quisses. It is encouraging that initial user trials report not only increased skills, but an increased appreciation for education.

- They also have a role to play in assessment as well as learning. In the United Kingdom, eVIVA is exploring innovative ways of assessing the Information and Communication Technologies (ICT) capabilities of students. Students compile online portfolios of their ICT work to show what they know and can do, the processes they have used, and the decisions they have made. Annotating their work gives them an opportunity to show their thinking. Teachers and other students can then provide feedback.

- They can support learning by allowing individuals involved in informal science to engage with the scientific enterprise. For example, citisens around the country can contribute their observations and counts of birds to support a national bird census, or participate in other scientist-citisen partnerships such as Salmon Watch programmes where volunteers contribute data from throughout a region.

Virtual Learning Environments

Gaming, Simulation, and Modeling

There is a growing use of virtual learning environments such as virtual resource centers and digital libraries, games, simulations, and models for work, play, entertainment, and scientific inquiry. Their potential for learning appears to be substantial as well.

Virtual Resource Centers

Virtual resource centers and digital libraries, for example, are known to impact the learning of students and teachers who continue to re-engage with them over time because they include opportunities for interaction, knowledge-building, and autonomy. In such contexts, the community of participants serves to support learners to stretch their understanding and to enable changes in their sense of possible selves that differs from those available in their local school.

It would not be unusual for a teacher who may not think she is strong in mathematics to become a lead teacher in mathematics and technology at another school. Similarly, students working with online interactive non-routine challenge problems in mathematics have been found to strengthen and deepen their mathematical thinking. Of note in each of these contexts is the role of interacting with others as a resource for developing knowledge.

For teachers, the community that emerges online is one that extends the possibilities of the local school district. On a heterogeneous site, this means not only a range of other teachers, but also tradespeople, mathematicians, scientists, researchers, educators, and parents from all over the world. There is a wide range of expertise and models of ways to think and talk about mathematics or science and resources that others have used effectively. In addition, the possibility of working alongside others grappling with similar issues in their classrooms, with the likelihood of finding oneself in the position of being both a learner and a supporter of others, is powerful for teachers.

A wide range of connections to others who are doing and thinking about subject content and pedagogy, coupled with the presence of interactive online services that have immediate possibilities for classroom use and/or discussion of applications to the classroom (e.g., technology-enhanced problems that fit reform practice and challenge students to stretch their understanding; question-and-answer services that enable students and/or teachers to think and talk with others about mathematics or mathematics pedagogy; an archives of like problems, already answered problems, and lesson plans), allow teachers to find and use materials that match the questions and needs that teachers bring to a virtual resource center or digital library.

For students, working with content online can provide direct contact and interaction with people whose content knowledge is rich and deep-for example, others who are interested in thinking at length about a mathematics issue that their teachers or peers are not. Technology-enhanced problems provide visual representations of mathematics that are not possible in pencil-and-paper formats; they also afford the possibility of interaction that allows the student to explore a concept-moving an axis or inserting a large number, for example-to see the impact of making such a decision. Importantly, students really like this form of online mathematics, and even weaker students are likely to persevere and develop a mental model of what the problem is asking.

Online interaction with others, such as that built into exchanges and feedback about the online problems, provides students with individualised feedback about their work, the kind of exchange in which others think with them, point them to related resources, and so on. A recent study of students working with technology-enhanced mathematics challenge problems, however, suggests that students who are best positioned to work with feedback about this type of problem online may be those who have an interest in mathematics.

Although they may like working with the online non-routine challenge problems, students with less, or no, interest in mathematics need support from their teacher to seriously engage in the feedback they receive. Gaming, simulation, and modeling. Games clearly motivate users in ways that much conventional instruction, including online non-routine challenge problems, does not. Some have observed that game players learn implicitly in the context of playing games, and are motivated to continue learning outside of the game in order to improve their game play. Game players are motivated to continue playing out of a sense of fun and enjoyment, characteristics that are often lost in formal instruction. Simulations and models help provide insights into scientific concepts and phenomena.

Difficult abstract concepts and large data sets can be accessed in ways that are more visual, interactive, and concrete. As such, simulations and models, and the games that incorporate them, have much to offer throughout a student's learning experience. Just as simulations and computational models play an increasing role in scientific and engineering practice, they can and should play a prominent role in learning. The challenge is to lay the scientific and technical groundwork to ensure that games and simulations have a positive influence on learning, not one that is negative or distracting.

To achieve these goals, a number of Cyberinfrastructure and research challenges must be addressed, including:

– Virtual learning environments need engines, authoring tools, and other modeling tools that make it easy for students, educators and other practitioners to create interactive services, games and simulations-quickly and at low cost. The current commercial game industry is characterised by proprietary platforms and licensing restrictions that create barriers for their educational applications. NSF and other government agencies can play a role in promoting interoperability standards, and in promulgating tools, platforms, and protocols for creating and modifying games.

– An infrastructure for data collection and analysis needs to be built into virtual learning environment engines to inform the development of Lifelong Learning Chronicles (LLCs). Instrumentation is lacking from commercial game engines, yet is critical for the Cyberinfrastructure in general. This infrastructure must support distributed data collection, both at home and in school, yet be secure, sensitive to privacy concerns, and tolerant of network connectivity problems in real-life educational settings.

- Cyberinfrastructure is needed to coordinate between virtual and real activities and resources. For example, learners need to be able to move seamlessly between game scenarios, Web-based resources relating to the concepts in the game scenarios, and online discussion groups and communities of learners employing these scenarios. Learner profiles and histories need to be portable between games and worlds, and through experiences spanning the learner's educational career, so that the learner need not start afresh with each new game-based learning experience.
- Tools and infrastructure that help bridge the gap between models and simulations used in scientific and engineering practice and those used in education are needed. Models used by practicing engineers and scientists tend to be highly detailed and require significant expertise to understand. However, if properly abstracted, simplified, annotated, and augmented, they can be transformed into learning resources as well.
- Cyberinfrastructure must address a range of digital divide concerns, including low-cost delivery options and interfaces that support all learners to access Web content, including those with diverse linguistic abilities and those with disabilities who need assistance in perceiving, understanding, navigating, and interacting with Web sites and applications.Novel interface modalities and participation structures are needed to support pre-K, primary, and secondary learners, as well as adult learners across the life span.

Although some evaluations of learning in virtual environments have been performed and othershave been proposed, more empirical research needs to be done, particularly of modern highly immersivegames and learning environments. The field of high school learning in virtual environments may also benefit fromlessons learned in the thriving field of simulated training environments, including those of the military, andin the convergence of work in medicine and virtual reality.

- Multiple researchers have observed that good games motivate learners to seek knowledge outside of the game in order to improve their performance within the game. Research in curriculum design and evaluation is needed to establish design principles for adapting curricula-to include interactive services such as online non-routine challenge problems, Web resources, integration of games and simulations-and to deepen our understanding of how to exploit the use of CELF to enable learners to work effectively with game-based and non-game-based materials.
- Studies must be conducted to assess the roles of motivation in online services and game-based learning that require self-regulation. Should design be undertaken such that learners are motivated to learn the concepts underlying a game, for example, as opposed to simply learning tricks for playing the game? This will require enhancement of our basic understanding of motivation and engagement at the neurobiological, cognitive, and sociocultural levels.
- Comparative analyses of learning where conjectured key features of interactive online services, gaming, and simulation environments are systematically removed, added, or altered in order to assess their impacts in relation to the strength and needs of learners, is important. This requires the flexible, reconfigurable virtual environment engines alluded to above, as well

as the instrumentation infrastructure to monitor, measure, and summarise learner performance using multiple media data streams and modalities, such as physiological sensing, not only traditional input device data. It also requires that support be provided to ensure effective use by learners, teachers and parents.

- A better understanding of the important role of virtual-environment-oriented "learning communities" is important. There is a common misconception that collaboration does not arise in connection with such virtual environments unless it is itself a multi-player world. Conversely, the effectiveness of virtual world online communities in promoting learning offers valuable lessons in how self-organised online communities can promote learning and the sharing of knowledge.
- Studies and theoretical frameworks that help to understand and critically evaluate the role of fidelity and immersiveness in virtual-world learning experiences, and in enhancing human task performances are important. In certain contexts, or for particular purposes, 'less' can be 'more.'
- Studies to assess the potential negative effects of game-oriented learning are also important. These include negative transfer from faulty simulation models, reinforcement of gender biases, the "rich-get-richer" effects in social networks and learning communities, emphasising action/"twitch" effects over reflection, and overemphasis of "eye candy" and other distracting details to the detriment of substantive learning.
- It is important to study the sociocultural differences in preferred gaming metaphors, graphical worlds, and avatars for different learner groups, and investigate

how to create game-based media that are sensitive to, and even can exploit, these factors without reinforcing negative stereotypes. Virtual reality environments for research enable nuanced social science research questions to be addressed concerning such learning-relevant topics as identity presentation and interactional consequences.

- Games and simulations raise new professional development issues for teachers. The new literacies involved in such media need to be developed for teachers, as well as methods that enable them to adapt, manage, and create virtual-world learning experiences and curricula for their purposes.

- The role of scaffolding in virtual learning environments needs to be carefully studied and developed. For example, games provide a range of scaffolding techniques, including simplified game modes with interaction that provides players with immediate feedback on their actions. Scaffolding can be embodied in characters, such as buddies and mentors, that are "embodied conversational agents" that engage in dialogic support for learners. These techniques should complement, and not duplicate, the kinds of scaffolding common in intelligent tutoring systems. Moreover, the role of scaffolding changes when learners become self-motivated to improve their own skills.

- The roles of narrative, stories, goal-based scenarios, and vignettes in virtual learning environments need to be properly understood. Story lines can make learning experiences more memorable and salient, but can also reduce the scope of learner control and can make it more difficult to introduce repetitive practice where it is needed and valuable.

Lifelong Learning Chronicles

Educational innovations and improvements are greatly hampered by the lack of sufficient quantitative data to properly assess their effectiveness and optimise their use. This is the motivation for a major thrust within the educational Cyberinfrastructure initiative to create a digital "Lifelong Learning Chronicle" (LLC) for each learner to collect and track the breadth and depth of that learner's experiences over his or her lifetime, and usefully indexes them for both personal reflective learning and certification purposes. The use of digital learning portfolios for personal ownership by learners has been a recurrent concept in recent history.

It was intimated in Vannevar Bush's pioneering 1945 "As We May Think" essay through his imagined digital notebooks for the scientist, which portended today's hypermedia systems and the World Wide Web. Massive reductions in the sise and cost of digital storage, now less than the cost of paper, make progress on this issue more tractable. Similarly, recent advances in machine learning and vision provide support for more robust person and object recognition, speech recognition, purposeful data-mining, and so on. In sum, the proposed LLC is an application of the frontiers of computing research.

LLCs can offer rich and compelling information to a wide variety of stakeholders. For example, individual learners would have the data they need to make informed decisions about their own learning-what knowledge they need to study, what learning resources are available that best align with their interests and learning style, what metacognitive skills could be improved, and what strengths and weaknesses they have that may influence future academic and employment choices. Learners will no longer have to take a single-shot, high-stakes assessment, but instead can benefit from continuous embedded assessments that provide both multiple opportunities to demonstrate their strengths and more rapid and accurate feedback to help in remediating their weaknesses.

However, the benefits of an LLC do not end with the learner-teachers, parents, administrators, researchers, policy makers, and society in general can all benefit from such a rich record. Teachers can guide their students' learning more effectively, professional development can be enhanced, and ultimately teaching can become more rewarding. Parents can also help their children learn, monitor their ongoing progress and make informed decisions about how to support their education. Administrators will have information for use in allocating resources appropriately so they can guide, support and reward teachers. Researchers can use LLCs to more deeply understand the processes involved in learning, particularly with respect to the new educational possibilities that Cyberinfrastructure affords.

As a result, they will be able to develop better Cyberinfrastructure learning technologies. Policy makers will have the opportunity to judge the effectiveness of new policies more quickly and accurately and respond accordingly. Workforce and training departments would be better able to account for workers' prior learning and develop individualised training. Industry would better understand what is required of the technologies when applied to the purposes of learning and education, and develop services that would better support them. Combining all these benefits, the better-educated and more adaptive workforce that will result from the use of LLCs should increase economic competitiveness.

For all these stakeholders, a major benefit of the continuous learner data collection is the possibility of much more rapid, informative, and accurate feedback and responsiveness than is possible with today's practices of occasional high-stakes and summative tests administered by teachers, instructors, and testing agencies during the school year. Data collection can go beyond traditional measures of domain content acquisition to include records of such factors as the processes learners have used in solving problems, information about whether learners are asking for help appropriately, and the way that learners may collaborate, cooperate and argue with each other. Faster cycles of feedback not only would foster better instructional decision making, but research in learning technology that is better focused on effective design and appropriate uses of that technology as well.

More generally, CELF should improve partnerships among these key education stakeholders and enable the tighter coupling of research, educational design, classroom practice and assessment, and industry's technical developments. Among other things, this would have implications for how NSFsupported learning sciences research and development is conducted, including that of NSF's Science of Learning Centers programme. Currently, most research projects are very loosely coupled and results rarely are cumulative in the knowledge that they produce. Too often learning technology research projects are far removed from classroom practice and its exigencies. The Cyberinfrastructure provides the opportunity for these projects and communities to work together more effectively.

The technical viability-as well as research challenges-of a digital LLC should be evident. Cyberinfrastructure technology developments will make it possible to store, search, and access records from LLCs. There has been continued exponential growth from 1990 to 2003 in hardware capabilities, including processor speed by a factor of 400, memory by a factor of 120, wireless speed by a factor of 18, and fiber channel bandwidth by a factor of 10,000. In five to seven years, mobile "phones" will have gigaherts processors and a gigabyte of memory. And as one UK report on "memories for life" notes, "The digital archive of even one person in the year 2019 is likely to consist of petabytes of linked images, documents and audio; the potential for extracting useful knowledge from this archive is stupendous, and only limited by our imagination."

The data-mining opportunities and challenges for LLCs are evident in considering even a basic data model. Consider the situation if and when each learner has a wireless handheld or laptop computer, and learning environments enable teachers and instructors to sustain regular learning conversations with their students that are technology-mediated in some measure. This trend emerging now with "classroom response and communication systems" in which teachers can pose questions (multiple choice and other designs) to which all their students can immediately respond, either anonymously or with identification.

These responses help teachers quickly gauge the students' conceptual understanding. Meanwhile, aggregate displays of student responses become visually available to the whole class through the teachers' projected computer display, enabling students to see the views of their peers. Archiving interactions, furthermore, permits study of the exchanges, providing a basis for assessment and feedback to the learner and the teacher, as well as needed information for service and/or gaming, simulation, and model refinement and development. For the 180 school days, each of 55 million U.S. K-12 students has about six periods of 50 minutes per class. If the teacher provides an occasion for each student to provide a response to his or her queries only once every five minutes of classroom time on such a technology platform, each student would have more than 10,000 such learning transactions in an academic year. This base model alone would generate 500 billion data points annually for U.S.

The LLC that the Cyberinfrastructure enables will extend beyond the walls of the classroom to include learner interaction data from a wide variety of information and communication technologies and media data streams. These include educational, performance, and entertainment technologies software (virtual laboratories, modeling tools, intelligent tutors, online assessments, and games), chat rooms, discussion boards, interactions with science museum exhibits, GPS-enabled cellular phones, and phone and grid conferences. This will require storing recordings of learner activities with both standard and novel recording techniques that capture synchronised data streams. The use of audio, video, scanners (e.g., for paper homework and tests), eye tracking, emotion sensing (e.g., galvanic skin response, or GSR), location/ proximity sensing (e.g., GPS), and brain imaging has tempting potential for deepening the scientific understanding of learners and how learner profiles and contextual factors contribute to learning processes and outcomes.

Cyberinfrastructure and research challenges include:

- Analysis and visualisation methods for distilling meaningful assessments from LLC data must be developed and presented in a form that learners, teachers, and other stakeholders can use. New methodologies of "visual analytics" will be needed for the analysis of enormous, dynamic, and complex information streams that consist of structured and unstructured text documents, measurements, images, and video. Significant human-computer interaction research will be required to best meet the needs of the various stakeholders. Stakeholders ought to be able to "drill down" into these assessments to see the justification for them in terms of learner performance. Analyses should be auditable, particularly when they have an impact on decision making, including college admissions and school-system performance assessments. These tools must be designed to give high priority to protecting the privacy and security of the data and users.

- There are many challenges and opportunities in collecting data for the LLC once it is understood that so much of learning occurs outside formal schooling. For example, how should educational games be instrumented to collect data, or children's interaction with mobile technologies be logged as they participate in field trips and visit museums, libraries, and other events? This information can provide for a deeper understanding of the way that informal learning supports formal schooling, but the technological and societal issues associated with its collection, analysis, and interpretation are more complex.
- The problems of protecting privacy and securing appropriate access permissions will need to be addressed. Fundamental computer science research will be needed to address such challenges. Social scientists will also need to address privacy and security issues from a policy perspective.
- How should learning environment design be re-conceptualised? It is inevitable that unforeseen data

patterns will emerge from the multiple synchronised data streams of learners and groups, given the present state of "data poverty,". Identification of emergent data patterns from these data streams could be defined as new "sensed quantities" in a classroom-properties of the classroom as a learning system that are changing over time. Such measures could be taken and used as inputs that would serve as triggers for dynamically changing the affordances of the learning environment.

– Identify relevant variables for analysis. What, for example, "counts" as scientific or mathematical thinking or literacy, and how can it be assessed online?

– Develop methods for comparative analysis of learner performance across LLC data nationwide. This is a major challenge for distributed computing, exacerbated by the fact that the necessary data are likely to be distributed in heterogeneous databases that may be intermittently disconnected from the Internet.

– Psychometric validation of LLC-based assessments is needed so they can be compared with conventional assessments, and complement and ultimately supplant them.

– How should the multiple data streams be synchronised to allow the rich descriptions that qualitative information provides to be coupled with precise quantitative accounts?

– Preservation and migration of data must be addressed. LLCs will have a lifetime that far exceeds the specific technologies used to store them. Moreover, as needs and capabilities change, LLC data formats and protocols are bound to change as well. Preservation and maintenance of LLC data will be a continual problem, and will require innovative solutions.

CYBERINFRASTRUCTURE FOR TEACHING

While the Internet has clearly influenced the opportunities available to a number of teachers, the working environment for many who have yet to connect to it may be unsatisfying professionally and lacking in intellectually enriching experiences, pathways for professional advancement, and sufficient resources for teaching their classes. Poor performance nationally and locally has led to increased demands for accountability and the record-keeping and testing that goes along with this. As these demands increase, the inadequate allotments of time and resources for professional development are further constrained, while new requirements such as technological competence and literacy are added.

The Cyberinfrastructure for education presents the opportunity to address many of the existing challenges. It will also extend already documented possibilities for teachers' professional development, while introducing new contexts demanding new modes of teaching and assessment. It can enable teachers to further develop their own knowledge and skills in the context of supporting them to work with these. In the K-12 arena, numerous studies and reports have documented the shortage of qualified teachers, related to poor preparation in pedagogical content knowledge and large turnover in the profession.

Consider the following scenario depicting an enriched classroom environment using Cyberinfrastructure:

Sherry is a tenth-grade science teacher. In preparing an earth sciences class, she downloads recent seismological data and incorporates them into a game-like, inquiry-based classroom activity. She feels a bit unsure about how to best structure the student groups and how to design her class activity, so she logs into her online professional development environment where her mentors provide advice and assistance. Her refined activity then becomes available to other teachers for use and adaptation. Along the way, Sherry learns more about the physics of shock wave propagation. Indeed, she learns to use a software tool that models this phenomenon.

In class, Sherry walks about the room, offering help and advice as students work through the activities. Because of the extended nature of the activity, students continue working collaboratively on the project at home. The environment includes a simulated scientist agent who can offer advice. As part of the activity, they use sensors connected to handheld devices to explore and collect vibration data in different physical environments. One student continues working on the problem during his after-school technology club. Other students in the club become engaged and suggest other resources for solving the problem.

Sherry, meanwhile, can assess students' progress and learning activity by accessing tools that visually display real-time analyses of their performance, attitudes, and the nature of their collaborative activity. She can consult her online assessment mentor to help her interpret these dynamically generated analyses, and offer tailored and developmentally appropriate feedback. Report generation software helps her prepare reports for parents and district administrators. These analyses can also help Sherry reflect on the quality of the instructional activity, student learning, and ways to implement improvements.

As described above, CELF can change the landscape by supporting student-directed inquiry using services and activities that provide scaffolds and generate Lifelong

Learning Chronicles (LLCs) that model and analyse a student's performance and learning activities. For teachers, the Cyberinfrastructure provides a means for connecting their students to new virtual communities of practice and, through this, expanding the teaching and mentoring resources available to students. Cyberinfrastructure can also change the nature of the classroom, enabling early pre-service access to students and classrooms, supporting them to target and develop particular competencies such as analysing students' efforts-for example, in the process of mentoring elementary students who are encountering online problems with their work-and connecting them to the range of possible ways to access other professional roles and activities.

In turn, these changes will introduce the need for new competencies in teaching. The availability of richer performance data will require that teachers integrate new skills in technology use, interpretation of student performance based on a wide range of data, and designing interventions in order to yield the desired improvements to education. As students can have more direct access online to current and highquality content and engaging experiences, the role of the classroom teacher as facilitator becomes even more important, helping students manage their online learning relationships and activities, articulate and share their learning, and assess their progress.

Online communities of learning have the potential to strongly support professional development. Early research suggests that participation in these communities supports a changed sense of identity and possibility because of their availability, comprehensiveness, and user-centered control over participation; their relative anonymity; the ease of movement within and between communities and roles; and the strength of engagement that comes from interest and access to strong community members. The ability to easily try out roles, from lurking participant to author or programme facilitator, provides motivation and opportunity for teachers to reflect on their professional activity, receive feedback and affirmation, and pursue advancement.

A "teacher" for every student and every student a teacher :Interestingly enough, this has been previously identified as a Grand Research Challenge for Information Systems. There are multiple emerging forms of providing more Socratic tutoring and interactive and individualised support more cost-effectively. These include interactive services, educational games, and intelligent tutors. There is also the opportunity to better tap the distributed expertise that is available in the learner population to enhance the learning that goes on at the system level. That is, any student can also serve as a teacher to other students and, as CELF develops, it will be easier to recognise which learners could serve as teaching resources for which of the other learners, pending their reputation authentication and availability and mechanisms for brokering such learning interchanges effectively. CELF could change the opportunities for a wider range of people to have more ways of playing a teaching role, bringing their expertise to students as education breaks out of the normal classroom structure.

In the higher education realm, new instructors, who often have little formal preparation as teachers, can become part of online communities where they can consult mentors, other new teachers and more experienced teachers, tradespeople using their discipline in the field, and others to find high-quality learning resources for their courses. This vision of teaching and teachers in the Cyberinfrastructure environment raises a number of research challenges. The research on learning and teaching in these different types of online and hybrid communities is very preliminary, and there is much to be understood. It is critical that strong models and communities of learners be developed to support teacher learning so that CELF supports the improvement of education rather than competing with it. This research must lead to design requirements and criteria for assessment that are used to develop platforms for collaboration and community development on which educational programme leaders can participate and refine their curricula and pedagogies.

Cyberinfrastructure teaching and research challenges include:

- Developing models of effective mentoring and approaches for supporting the development of identitychanged learning in online professional development environments. Addressing issues of incentives, release time, recognition, and rewards for participation in such environments.
- Developing models for supporting sustainable, productive online communities.
- Supporting the meaningful integration of Cyberinfrastructure skills and resources (e.g., networked instruments, data sets, visualisation, and modeling software) into formal learning environments.
- Providing the means for harnessing the potential of Cyberinfrastructure resources for teachers

  to engage in developing and deepening subject content knowledge and pedagogical content knowledge.
- Understanding teaching as a complex work environment. This includes providing effective tools, mentors, and support in teaching environments with integrated student learning, performance, assessment, and feedback.

- Developing robust models of teaching and curriculum development that prepare all kinds of students to work in the Cyberinfrastructure world, including models for designing interdisciplinary and collaborative curricula.
- Fostering teaching across boundaries: supporting students' transitions in learning from virtual learning environments with formal and non-formal learning environments. Developing standards supporting the transparent portability of information about user capabilities across contexts. Developing social and technical theory that supports seamless navigation between life spheres.

Communities of Learners

The virtual world has expanded the communities of learning in which students and teachers can participate and the roles that virtual environments can play in the educational system. Even more, communities of learning are situated in a context of social networking that has already been and will continue to be transformed by Cyberinfrastructure. In the virtual world, social networking functions can enable learners to aggregate into communities of interest and evolve into communities of learning or practice. We need to understand the formation of these communities and ways to facilitate the contribution of cybersocial networking to the learning and engagement of students and teachers. Additionally, social capital influences who participates and the focus of community activity, which leads to various learning outcomes for different types of learners and groups.Virtual communities of learning also offer the promise of bridging the worlds of work and education.

Cyberinfrastructure will make it possible for students in school settings to be more directly engaged with life beyond the classroom, and to observe and interact with communities of professionals and others who develop products and results that matter, both within and outside of their communities. Additionally, experience with virtual communities of learning directly prepares students for working in such environments outside of school-based education. Much work needs to be done to manage layers of participation that enable students and others to participate, at levels appropriate to their interest and competencies, in ways that do not intrude on the work of the others yet make their results and activity accessible as appropriate.

Virtual communities of learning can help address many of the issues raised above about the need to retain qualified and talented teachers and support them in their professional practice. They can provide personal support as well as access to professionally interesting conversations and resources; connections to practicing scientists and education researchers; and more opportunities for advancement than the local context often can offer.

CELF research challenges include:

- Managing the need for large-scale, robust production systems upon which practitioners can rely and researchers can do research, coupled with the ongoing need for innovative experiments.
- Developing shared standards and specifications to enable the collection and analysis of data about communities of learning.
- Understanding and planning for educating teacher practitioners to use Cyberinfrastructure for learning collaboratively and across groups.

- Understanding the affordances of the virtual context for individuals and groups to develop multiple competencies and various senses of belonging that they and others can manage to construct, and adapt the learning environments to their needs.
- Understanding how social capital influences the participation of different types of learners and, in turn, how various forms of participation impact learning.
- Identifying and learning to assess criteria for engagement and success within communities of learning.Integrating across different forms of assessment data, such as interviews and observation, discourse and conversation analysis, log analysis, and performance evaluations.
- Developing effective community feedback mechanisms for "reading" member engagement and perspectives and facilitating various forms of decision making.
- Understanding how access, availability, and ubiquity affect the development of Communities of Learners enabled by CELF.
- Understanding how pedagogical content knowledge and related principles should influence the design of infrastructures to support communities of learning.
- Understanding how to support cross-project collaboration and fertilisation. Understanding how Cyberinfrastructure can bridge projects both within and across traditional disciplines. Understanding how projects move from pilots to large-scale efforts and from grant-funded to sustainable.
- Understanding the global nature of Cyberinfrastructure. Although the Internet and much of industry

are already internationally oriented, education in the United States is remarkably parochial. Cyberinfrastructure can help bridge learners across countries (pilots, and small-scale individual efforts) and make it possible (time zones notwithstanding) for class projects to consist of team members worldwide, and to bring in experts from around the world.

Establishing CELF will involve far more than making scientific data sets available online. It should provide the means for ubiquitous collection and utilisation of learning-related data, in a manner that respects privacy and control concerns. It should provide tools and resources that enable learners at all levels, as well as teachers and those serving educative roles, to exploit the potential of the Cyberinfrastructure in equitable and productive ways. CELF should provide access to science and engineering resources, but in a form that learners and educators can effectively use in meaningful and tailored ways. New forms of professional development are required to enable educators to contribute to and make effective use of this Cyberinfrastructure.

Without a concerted and focused effort, the vision of CELF as a meaningful educational implement will not happen on its own. Risks include:

1) isolating education and learning from a socio-technological revolution that has already fundamentally altered the scientific process and has great potential benefits in this realm;

2) depriving learners at all levels from engaging with rich, motivating and tailored learning experiences that prepare them for work in an information economy;

3) bypassing a major chance at attracting new talent to the community of teaching professionals;

4) missing an opportunity for building balanced, continuous, and context-sensitive assessments;

5) accumulating fragmented, disconnected, incoherent data sets that cannot be shared for the purposes of informing both stakeholders and education researchers; and

6) adopting a narrow focus on analysing and interpreting only data that are easy to collect.

Efforts to develop standards and code-sharing would address some risks. Assuming that the very difficult privacy and security issues can be addressed, then use of more sophisticated data collection methods can also help address some of these risks. However, even with the development of standards, methods are needed to combine legacy and contemporary databases from the various sources in which they reside, such as school districts, game systems, classroom computers, and learners' personal computing and mobile devices such as cellular phones.

Cyberinfrastructure research will have a minimal impact on educational practice. CELF needs to improve learning for all learners and not just the few. Research must address the fundamental requirement that this infrastructure will enable more inclusive and accessible education. Moreover, it is unlikely that the private sector will fill the gap, given that the current Cyberinfrastructure involves a multitude of incompatible protocols and standards, with little attention to interoperable instrumentation. Consequently, policy changes are required both to fully implement educational Cyberinfrastructureand to properly exploit it. The following are some of the areas where educational Cyberinfrastructure haspolicy implications.

- *Privacy, Security, and Integrity*: One clear example of demands on Cyberinfrastructure, raised particularly with regard to the handling of human data (as opposed to, say, astronomical data), is privacy. Under most conditions of use, data on human subjects and student classroom performance must be anonymised for scientific or public use. There are significant challenges for anonymisation, and a community of data privacy and privacy technology researchers has emerged. Further challenges follow from the fact that different stakeholders may have different access needs for data about student or classroom performance.

- *Preserving and Safeguarding Data*: Educational Cyberinfrastructure will collect and store huge amounts of data about learner performance. In order to fully reap the benefits of these data, they must be stored and maintained over a long period of time. This requires institutional commitments to maintain these data sets. Moreover, steps must be taken to maintain the integrity of data once they are collected. The data collection process must have sufficient redundancy and safeguards in case of hardware malfunction or operator error. Even seemingly innocuous actions such as software upgrades could cause data sets to be overwritten and lost.

- *Utilisation*: The educational Cyberinfrastructure of CELF will be beneficial only if it is well utilised. Data must be collected and saved, and not discarded. Educational technologists can strive to make educational Cyberinfrastructure as easy to use as possible, but maintaining it still requires commitment at all levels. Otherwise data are likely to be fragmentary and easily lost. Where the Cyberinfrastructure requires new types of data to be collected, such as video recordings and self-assessment instruments, policies must be in place to ensure compliance. These may be of less concern for government-funded research projects in which researchers are available to ensure compliance, but are critical as educational institutions move to adopt CELF for their own uses in mission-critical applications.

- *Equity of Access and Ability to Use the System*: Equity issues must remain a central concern in the Cyberinfrastructure R&D agenda. Currently, students do not have equal access to high-quality instructional resources, nor do they have equal access to highly qualified teachers, particularly for higher-level science and mathematics courses. With the increasing diversity of native languages in the nation's schools and workplaces, the challenges of meeting multilingual needs are an important aspect of this access problem. Ensuring that materials are designed to address the learning challenges of underserved populations and communities is a national imperative.
- *Ownership*: In order for educational Cyberinfrastructure to make the transition into widespread use, issues of ownership and control must be kept in mind. First of all, learners and parents should have rights to control who has access to data that are collected about them. Yet it is ultimately the educational institutions that are responsible for ensuring that the data are properly collected and maintained.
- *Educating the Public About Policies*: The educational processes envisioned by CELF require the involvement and concurrence of the public at large. The public needs to be informed of the potential benefits of the new technologies and methods, and of the protections

and safeguards built in to ensure integrity and proper use. Public involvement will be required to set priorities for the use of CELF, and public support will be necessary for its proper implementation.

– *Evidence-Based Assessment and Decision Making*: CELF will make possible new methods for assessing the performance of learners, teachers, schools, and school districts. It is incumbent upon the research community to ensure that these assessments are reliable so they can be justifiably employed by decision makers at all levels. They need to provide a picture of learner performance that is as accurate as possible, in a way that resists attempts to distort results by "teaching to the test." Once this has been accomplished, policy makers need to embrace these new assessment methods, and use them to take steps to improve the educational process. Only then will the revolutionary potentials of the Cyberinfrastructure for Education and Learning for the Future be achieved.

7

Integrated Technology in Teaching

Technology use in classroom presents an ongoing challenge in education. With few exceptions, most professional development programmes have not provided teachers with the knowledge or experience to begin to use computer technology in their classroom in the same manner as other tools, such as the whiteboard, posters, manipulatives and text.

Technology integration no longer involves only the knowing of the computer related technologies and software—it involves the way teachers and students approach learning. The amount of primary and secondary information available to the classroom and how that information can be organised, thought about and presented requires new skills for both teachers and students. The use of computer related technology provides opportunity for the construction of new knowledge from different sources, the organisation of qualified information, making meaning of information for and presenting that information to a larger community.

Over the years in higher education, professional development for teachers in the area of technology integration has focused on the technology itself and the software. Unfortunately, without good technology integration models or knowledgeable leadership, teachers found themselves struggling to understand the hardware, with little energy left to integrate the technology into the learning environment.

Historically, technology facilitators focused on the bells and whistles of software leaving participants with a false sense of knowledge of the potential of the software for teaching and learning. The attractions that computers initially presented for teachers were as varied those who attempted to use them. Teachers must understand the computer applications more completely to use the computer a tool for learning. The challenge becomes one of how to best prepare prospective teachers and inservice teachers for teaching and learning with technology.

Prospective teachers often come to the public or private schools with a basic understanding of computer applications and not of the big picture of the possibilities for technology integration. Further, according to the US National Center for Educational Statistics survey data approximately 20% of teachers entering the educational system felt prepared to implement educational technology in their classrooms.

New teachers entering the educational system do not possess the depth of understanding to create classrooms as a model of technology integration despite greater emphasis on technology learning in higher education. In addition to the challenges with technology that new teachers face, inservice teachers experience similar concerns. According to Duhaney, the results of a national survey indicated that a majority of teacher respondents had some training in technology but only 20% felt comfortable using computers. Additionally, respondents reported difficulty in understanding how to use technology to support an engaging and meaningful learning environment. Therefore, the burden of educating teachers to a more global understanding of technology literacy falls to the school system itself.

The US Association of State Boards of Education highlighted the critical need for adequate professional learning in technology use in order to achieve enhanced learning opportunities for students. Yet, many higher education organisations continue to fall short of providing comprehensive training for the classroom teacher beyond the software applications.

BARRIERS OF TECHNOLOGY INTEGRATION

There are many reasons for the lack of deeper knowledge of technology integration by teachers, including teacher apathy, district budget limitations, lack of leadership, and lack of availability of training. Yet, the greatest inhibitor to technology integration is time. It takes many hours of use and planning to learn the possibilities of a computer software application and have time to explore possibilities for integration.

Teachers' knowledge of the software application is limited consequently; applying it to a meaningful learning context in the classroom is a difficult task. This process needs direction and support and must be a collaborative effort using the combined knowledge base of classroom teachers, administrators, curriculum support personnel ar technology facilitators. Therefore, lack of support, fim leadership, and collaboration and knowledge of tl curriculum content leads to lack of efficacy teachers has regarding how to integrate technology into the classroom.

Additionally, the evolution of technology created other challenges for teachers as they struggled to 'keep up' with the speed of technology changes.

The evolution of the computer, the demands of society, the school community, and the political control of education by textbook companies blurred the teachers' conceptions of the purpose of technology in teaching. Teachers viewed computer technology as a disconnect from the curriculum. A disconnect means that teachers see no relevance between what the students need to know and what they can construct, find or ponder with computer technology. Additional challenges to technology integration occurred as educators envisioned computers as a new instructional management tool.

The emergence of networked computers and the acceptance of the textbook driven curriculum, provided a gateway for the adoption of Integrated Learning Systems (ILS). Many district superintendents viewed the ILS systems as a panacea: the answer to the community calling for more technology use as well a response to teachers resisting computer use in the classroom. The need for professional development for teachers decreased, since paraprofessionals in many cases were responsible for the labs.

While students received their computer experience in the ILS labs, some teachers perceived this as a reason or excuse for not using the computer for instruction. In the late 1980s and early 1990s, leaders in technology, such a Bank Street College, Massachusetts Institute of Technology and Seymour Papert began to focus on technology as a tool for inquiry. Programmes such as Logo, the Voyage of the Mimi, and Windows on Science videodisks, promoted the ideas and concepts of inquiry based learning. The combinations of equipment needed to use these programmes in the classroom was so complex, that teachers did not use them or abandoned them unless the teacher was "wire aware", or in other words hardware literate. The few teachers that had an understanding of the possibilities and had a vision for the potential of technology at that time often could not acquire shared visions of the school administration or their peers. Adding to the inhibitors of technology use was the problem of the technology in classrooms and labs failing to function.

Teachers did not have the knowledge to make repairs, and computers sat lifeless. Students ultimately had limited access to computers, training was insufficient and little connection between curriculum and technology existed. Unfortunately, it is this mistreated past of 'disconnect' that remains in the minds of many teachers and administrators when technology is addressed in schools today. It was not until the availability of the Internet in K-12 education that began to increase teachers' interest in technology uses. Those teachers, principals and curriculum leaders who saw the potential of the technology continued to gather knowledge and become evangelists of the movement to have computer technology make a difference in learning.

Research conducted by Apple Classrooms of Tomorrow (ACOT) argued that students could learn better and faster when using a computer to learn According to ACOT, students could be more motivated if computers were available for use as a tool to facilitate inquiry learning and representation of their knowledge and understandings. Educators today need to separate themselves from the past and accept technology as an integral part of the education of students in the 21st century. With resources exploding, lesson ideas available, and student activities at their fingertips teachers must embrace the accessibility of information on the World Wide Web. Many teachers are becoming more responsive to learning about the computer and its use in the classroom versus labs only. However, the largest problem that remains in education today is connecting technology to curriculum content and to the learning processes. Schools need a staff development model that assists teachers in understanding technology as a tool for connecting curriculum content to learning processes. Institutions of higher learning should consider the same model as prospective teachers are prepared to enter the teaching profession.

Mapping the Curriculum

When facing the problem of getting teachers to effectively use technology for teaching and learning in the classroom, we need to start from where the teachers are in their own understandings. We want teachers to view technology as a transparent tool in the classroom. Teachers need to recognise technology as an instrument in their tool chest for teaching and learning. According to Rudnesky, computers need to be part of daily classroom activities to make technology transparent. Moreover, we believe that teachers should not have students involved with technology for 'technology's sake 'only.'

For technology integration to occur, we propose it is necessary to initially understand and organise the content of the curriculum by grade level. Teachers need to recognise what they are teaching across a yearlong curriculum. The process used for this purpose is curriculum mapping. Heidi Hayes Jacobs, a leading authority of curriculum mapping, refers to the process as putting together the big picture. Jacobs expressed the concept that teachers should organise the curriculum and connect the resulting instruction in the classroom in a way that is logical and meaningful for students. Jacobs discouraged teachers from focusing solely on the content of the curriculum, but to teach concepts that across units, even perhaps across the entire year. One of the reasons for mapping the curriculum is to avoid the static nature of curriculum development that has plagued education historically.

Teachers need to talk about curriculum through a dynamic process. The process of curriculum mapping provides a forum for substantive conversations among teachers regarding important decisions about content, instructional delivery, alignment, and pacing concerns eventually 'digging deeper' into more conceptual understandings of learning processes and curriculum organisation. This begs the argument that curriculum development should not exist within a traditional 3-5 year cycle that does not provide ongoing dialogue within professional learning forums.

Teachers require continued discussions to plan effectively for the future learning needs instead of responding only to the high stakes testing demands of today. Another reason for curriculum mapping is to improve communication among teachers, administrators, parents and community. Communication between levels, buildings and courses has become increasingly important as accountability forces us to monitor and adjust teaching to improve student learning. Accountability requirements result in tracking the students progress across years and levels, therefore, schools must pay closer attention to what, how and when they are teaching content. Curriculum maps provide a structure to examine possible gaps and overlaps in our educational delivery systems.

Consolidation of resources, space, time and materials is another reason to map curriculum. As communication occurs regarding common themes, content, topics and assessments then teachers begin to identify resources, materials and other needs as necessary teaching tools. Teachers are better able to combine efforts in organising and sharing their needs when the curriculum map provides instructional focus. For example, if 5th grade teachers understand that they will be teaching a unit on exploration, they are better able to collaborate on lessons and other resources. This collaboration may include but not be limited to assigning different teachers to different tasks such as organising media center time to collect reference books, finding and bookmarking Internet sites and creating learning centers. This type of collaboration and consolidation of resources is not only limited to a building level but can expand to include other 5th grade teachers across the district.

Curriculum mapping is a way to meet both the needs of the students and the requirements of the district and state as well. We propose that the process of curriculum mapping extend beyond the basic curriculum content students must know. Teachers must correlate the learning processes students need in order to apply their acquired knowledge to more global understandings. If teachers use curriculum mapping to identify what skill students need to apply to learning, the missing process skills can be determined. For example, if first grade students need to learn about life cycles, the teachers must determine learning processes that best facilitate the students' understanding such as observation, reflection, data collection, and sequencing. These learning processes demand an inquiry approach that may involve project based learning, mini quests, distance learning experiences, an off-site extension or combination of any of these approaches. Teachers are able to map instructional delivery approaches, along with the digital age skills such as technology literacy, communication, inventive thinking and problem solving across the curriculum and grade level.

Developing Curriculum Maps

Teachers who enter into the process of curriculum mapping or content 'uncoverage' develop a better understanding of their curriculum. Teachers must first decide what is taught and when through a series of substantive conversations. Teachers also make discoveries across grade levels that there are mismatches in curriculum alignment. Through this dialogue, realisations occur relative to content that has not been covered, hidden curriculum or pet projects, and pacing issues. Following several sessions of dialog, we posit that the next steps become critical to the curriculum mapping process.

- *Step 1*: Look for connections within the curriculum that teachers implement throughout the year. (e.g. systems (government, body, space—connecting both science and social studies required content)
- *Step 2*: Select a theme; or topic (e.g. communities, systems, exploration).
- *Step 3*: Select a conceptual thread—change over time; likenesses /differences; interdependency. Teachers identify a big idea or enduring understanding at this step which serves as an overarching organiser for the unit. Focus on concepts beyond the 'facts' is essential for higher order thinking.

  Teachers soon discover that some concepts weave across several subject areas. For example, the concepts of change, patterns, interdependence, symmetry, system and movement can be examined in many subjects or serve to unite the subject areas. For example, the theme of conflict relates to the content of social studies (war), literature (among characters) and science (survival). Another example is the theme of patterns or change over time found in literature (rhyme; rhythm, repetition), math (patterns all around us), science (pattern in life cycles), music and art (patterns in style, texture, tempo rhythm).

Teachers might incorporate reading and music as they see how rhythms, harmony, repetition all relate to early reading skills. Teachers discover a similar connection as they consider how classification, patterns, likenesses and differences are interconnected in the area of math and science. As these connections emerge it becomes clear how teachers may find one or two concepts to unite a unit or theme.

- *Step 4*: Identify district or state curriculum standards, benchmarks and appropriate assessments Teachers should be able to determine the core knowledge expressed in the standards and benchmarks.
- *Step 5*: Develop 2-5 essential questions based on this core knowledge. Jacobs defined an essential question as the essence of what students will examine and learn in the course of their study. The questions should be of different kinds according to Erickson.
  - Factual—"Name the parts of a plant"
  - Conceptual—"What benefits are plants to the environment?"
  - Philosophical -" "Should rain forests be protected?"
- *Step 6:* Determine appropriate assessments of the students learning at the conclusion of the unit/theme

study. Assessment should drive instruction and allow for differentiation based on the needs of students.

- *Step 7*: Determine the learning processes. Identify the processes needed to best learn or acquire the information.
- *Step 8:* Establish method of inquiry. Choose instructional methodology-Project based; problem based; learning center base, collaborative project or a combination of these processes
- *Step 9:* Develop lessons, activities, projects that connect with the topic or theme developed. In education, teachers often start with this step. The problem with starting with lessons and activities is one of not understanding if they lead to understanding of the content and concepts.

Curriculum in general can be unrelated or fragmented. However, through the curriculum mapping process, teaching for meaning and understanding occurs. Students focus on 'big ideas' and use higher-level thinking and problem solving skills. This approach helps teachers focus on essential learning and promote active, inquiry learning. In these classrooms, teachers encourage students to explore substantive learning from a variety of perspectives and sources. Additionally, curriculum integration through the curriculum mapping processes can make the content more understandable to students and more meaningful. Teachers begin to see how technology supports inquiry learning contrary to methods that are more traditional. Student and teachers use of technology begins to develop into a third dimension of the initial curriculum map Teachers not only have their yearly curriculum mapped through this process, but also identify technology integration possibilities. The identification of meaningful technology connections to the curriculum must come from their own experiences gained from professional development sessions, professional reading and research or a more knowledgeable other such as a technology consultant.

For example, a second grade teacher may begin to see that it is a natural for his/her students to use Kidspirations to compare and contrast a variety of topics in the curriculum. This level of teacher knowledge and process may seem a small step forward in the development of technology integration. However, it is a needed step for teachers to understand the functions that technology potentially serves. Once teachers begin to acknowledge the learning processes that technology can facilitate and locate additional resources they continued to develop their related maps.

Collaboration, risk-taking, and sharing of resources are critical to the change process. Recognition of adult levels of learning is essential to the delivery of support services to teachers Professional development must be an ongoing process and on an as-needed basis.

The curriculum mapping process, an understanding of what students must know, and best practice methodologies are all critical to the teachers' understanding of the technology 'fit' and the capabilities of technology to enhance the learning process.

Technology increases the self-directed learning opportunities for both students and staff. In the overall process of curriculum mapping and technology alignment, technology does not drive instruction; curriculum is the driving force in the application of technology and learning. We all know that students today face rapidly changing technologies and that 'global understandings' are no longer busswords. Knowledge regulated to textbooks, random

Internet 'research', ideas from the teachers connected to the expectation of coverage from standards and benchmarks all limit the learning possibilities of our students.

Basic skills for the students of the 21st century skills will include basic literacy in the subject areas but in addition, students also need basic scientific, economic, and digital literacy. In addition, students need to be literate in visual and informational literary, global, and cultural differences. The students of the 21st century also need to be inventive in their thinking, be able to communicate their ideas in published form and verbally, and to use the tools of the 21st century for learning, communication, and problem solving.

8

Online Teaching

Technologies alter perceptions of time, place and space, and thereby change what is understood and lived as human embodiment. The shift from oracy to literacy some 3000 years ago, for instance, revolutionised forms of agency and sociality by allowing people to communicate across distances of place and time. In a similar way, the current semiotic shift to electronic visuality and virtuality is generating new forms of communication and community, including those that occur in classrooms.

Policies, pedagogies and practices of education programs today need to be learner-directed, collaborative and customised. An online course taught in a pre-service teacher education course where the curriculum and pedagogy converge to model the principles of teacher with technology, student with teacher, and student with student that are taught in its content. Online teaching for collaborative learning that occurred around, with and through the Internet, the curriculum, and the students' engagement with the course's requirements. Media studies help students understand how the mass media construct social realities, values and identities through the creation of meaning and desire in text. The curricular focus of media and cultural studies courses are those texts and images that are relevant to an increasingly diverse and media-saturated student population. Tutorials are also delivered in a combination of face-to-face and electronic modes. Students meet once a week in the technology studios to participate in the e-tutorial discussions, and to work on their assignments and webpages.

Attendance at tutorials is compulsory, but students come and go at will. The tutorial groups are also assigned to an electronic email list that forms a virtual tutorial or online discussion group. E-tutorials provide an electronic forum for discussion of the course readings, the lectures and assignments. At the macro level, many features of the Media and Technologies classroom were different from conventional university teaching settings. For example, with the exception of the lectures, the students' work took place not in a classroom but in a computer laboratory, at any of the library's terminals, or at the students' homes.

Microanalyses of the social and physical space in which group activities occur explicate the relations of the interactions taking place. The ideological function of spatiality is fundamental in teaching and learning environments where discursive practices and social relations intersect directly with the axes of knowledge and power. In traditional classrooms, the distribution of students' bodies in rows, the unobstructed gaze of the teacher, and the authority deployed by her/him creates knowledge. This, in turn, provides the means for the exercise of power. Power is exercised through "discipline," which trains and corrects.

Contrary to the Marxist position on power as a negative *thing* wielded from the top down and legitimated by false ideologies, Foucault views power in terms of social relations at the local or micro level. Because it constructs knowledgeable and socially useful individuals, power is positive and productive. The promotion of collaborative learning was central to the design and organisation of Media and Technologies in Education. The organisational principle of this classroom was cooperation rather than competition. This sociality extended to off-campus contact, where students met in colleges and flats to work together to meet assignment deadlines. In a study of online personal networks in a distance education program, Haythornthwaite similarly established the importance of informal contact and communication. In the classes she investigated, frequent and multiplex social ties of either face-to-face or virtual proximity were central to student motivation, class participation, and "anytime, anyplace work and social bonds." The specificities of institutional context, curricular resources and pedagogical practices in technology-mediated learning environments militate against the formulation of generic outcomes or lessons that are globally transferable. Nevertheless, the provision of information on the insights gained by this group of teachers through the changes they made to their course may ease the design and implement process for others.

A recent technical development, for example, is the adoption of the bulletin board software application, Web CT, for e-tutorials. The teaching staff anticipates that this will alleviate difficulties associated with the tediousness of the less flexible, asynchronous method used previously. A recent upgrade of computer laboratory equipment also should enable the students to focus their collaborative energies on task related intellectual issues rather than on technical problems. In turn, this should reduce student anxiety levels induced by negative encounters with technology, many of which previously were a product of inadequacies in university infrastructure. Finally, a reduction in time spent talking "at" students with the reallocation of one of the two hours of lecture time to tutorial activity will maximise opportunity for hands-on collaborative activity.

The nature of the collaborative learning that occurred with and around online technologies in one course of a teacher education program. Teachers create learning conditions in which understanding is possible, and students are obligated to capitalise on those conditions. The pedagogical conditions in this class comprised hybrid social practices combining traditional methods (e.g., face-to-face lecturing) with new theory (e.g., constructivism), relevant content (e.g., media and cultural studies) and new information technologies (e.g., email and World Wide Web). Hence, the convergence of instructional design and online pedagogies of Media and Technologies in Education modeled the kinds of learning and teaching that course content about the technologies promoted.

The digital technologies used here enabled a diminution of teacher-student contact and an increase in student independence and interdependence. Whilst the teaching staff imparted information and knowledge to students via conventional didactic means, the tutors used a facilitative pedagogical approach rather than a transmission method. The data indicated that more generative learning occurred through self-directed group work in the tutorials and Open Access sessions than from listening and note-taking in lectures. As the students realized the benefits of working with others in the laboratory class, they cooperated to achieve their tasks and overcome the problems that arose in the achievement of that goal. The inevitability of interdependence led some of them to be critical of their personal, individualistic work styles. Learning in this class occurred not so much through a body of content to be mastered but in and through the process of achieving a complex, technology-mediated group task.

Student course evaluations, assignments and assessment showed that the course design and delivery provided most of the students an understanding of the concepts and practices of media studies and multiliteracies. As each complication arose, students cooperated to identify and resolve the issue within the context of that particular literate or technological domain. Opportunity to collectively verbalise difficulties and to reflect on the progress of their understanding of that difficulty, provided students with reasoned, collective and coherent insight to the problem space. The skills, techniques and knowledges acquired arose out of the demands of the context, whether that was solving a problem in relation to their homepage, or posing questions to the e-tutorial discussion group. This instance of authentic, engaged sociality and democratic spatiality generated the kinds of independent and interdependent attitudes to learning that are essential in the networked and communications-oriented classrooms and communities of Information Age.

Knowledge-building Community Model

For over a thousand years universities operated on the assumption that information would be stored centrally and scholars would come to this central store of knowledge and collaborate to produce more information that would be stored at this site. Modern storage of information in digital form and the use of telecommunications allows scholars and students to access information from any location that connects to the Internet. Thus, instead of people coming to the information, people now can have the information come to them. When information comes to people via the World Wide Web, there are many potential benefits. Such benefits include: direct access to a broad range of information; access to learning environments outside normal lecture and tutorial times; greater opportunity for experiencing a variety of instructional strategies including small group discussion and collaborative projects; and exposure to a forum for expressing and sharing ideas.

While the technology allows greater access to stored knowledge and distributed personal knowledge, some researchers claim that education that is based entirely on such technology can contribute to a loss of community. During the study, the communication capabilities of the Web were used to support the development of preservice teacher understanding of the values, norms, and habitual ways of seeing which belong to the teaching profession. This learning process relied upon effective integration into a community of practice and was facilitated through immersion in the discourse of the community. Learning processes that are "grounded in talk" can stimulate higher order thinking skills by providing a context and mechanism for explanation, justification and reason. Therefore, learner interaction with instructors and other learners becomes essential if they are to master the concepts and skills associated with their profession.

Both the face-to face and on-line communities were needed to support a new approach to initial education called a 'knowledge-building community' (KBC). The KBC model that was adopted consisted of three interacting sources of learning:

- Community-learning (CL) which involved students, university and school facilitators sharing knowledge as a community;

- School-based learning (SL) which involved the students in authentic school contexts;
- Problem-based learning (PBL) which involved students working in groups to investigate problems.

The collaborative technologies used were designed to provide students with communication tools that they could use to engage in informal processes of knowledge sharing and construction. Many studies for computer mediated communication (CMC) noted that students desire more face-to-face interaction. That CMC can supplement face-to-face teaching by providing discussion forums that are non-threatening and allow for learner control of communications and learner involvement in topic negotiation. CMC tools allow individuals to maintain links with their community of practice and to take advantage of the scaffolding that is provided by a dynamic social context.

The purpose of the KBC project was to provide students enrolled in an initial teacher education course with an alternative pathway to professional socialisation through the formation of a Knowledge Building Community (KBC). Such professional socialisation occurs through the transmission of values, norms, and habitual ways of seeing which belong to particular occupations and shape the way that people conduct their work and establish themselves in the larger social world.

Problem-based Learning for Curriculum Development

Problem based learning (PBL) is a curriculum development and an instructional strategy designed to challenge students. Originally developed for medical schools, it was seen to be 'tailor made' for medicine because it provided advantages for both acquisition of knowledge and development of problem solving skills in patient care. A curriculum that makes use of PBL encourages and motivates students to 'learn to learn'. Above all, PBL challenges students to take charge of their education by involving students in small groups to solve 'real world' problems. During this process, students develop skills of negotiation, communication, and collaboration. The emphasis is placed on 'real world' problems which are 'ill-structured'. Ill-structured problems have the following characteristics:

(1) they require more information to understand the problem,

(2) the problem definition changes as new information is added to the situation,

(3) many perspectives can be used to interpret information, and

(4) there is no absolutely 'right' answer.

The main reason why the Faculty of Education at the University of Wollongong wanted to use a PBL approach within their KBC was to respond to recurrent themes emerging from studies which sought to follow-up graduates of teacher education courses. One was that many students reported that they left university with feelings of being under-prepared for life in classrooms and confused by what confronted them when they arrived at schools. The other was that schools which employed them reported that a majority of recent graduates were unaware of how school and classroom cultures operated, and were unable to see the relationships between what they studied at university and how it could be translated into classroom practice that produced effective student learning. This situation arises because most teacher education courses present a fragmented view of learning and this can hinder the development of professional socialisation of preservice teachers. There are three reasons for this:

- teacher education courses often split the study of learning into independent subjects focussing on psychological and sociological aspects and this can lead to a narrow and fragmented view of learning;

  the organisation of these subjects is often based on the delivery of decontextualised, theoretical knowledge that has little relevance to trainee teachers.

  practice teaching occurs in isolation from the university context.

Brown and Duguid argue that this type of learning makes use of knowledge that must be "stolen". They contend that the most important knowledge is that which cannot be taught and students must find ways to steal it from their educational environment. Such knowledge *habitus* - conditioning, a feel for the game, a disposition, the durable systems of schemata of perception, apprehension, and action that result from the institution of the social and the individual. During the second part of the KBC course, which ran for nine weeks, students attended their host school for two days per week and attended university for one or two days per week. When they were in schools they had two main roles. One was to be an effective teaching associate and the other was to be what we called 'an educational anthropologist'. The role of an educational anthropologist was to 'live' within the school community and to 'steal knowledge' that would help them to develop an understanding of the culture of their schools and of the actions of the children and teachers that they observed. Thus they needed to work with a number of teachers and allied professionals who acted as 'informants' about their profession and the culture of the school. As they gathered this information they would share it with others in their community.

Community Learning for Curriculum Development

Before problem-based learning (PBL) and school-based learning (SL) could be attempted it was necessary to build a learning community (LC). The KBC project was designed so that community learning would support the students as they embarked upon the other two sources of learning. Thus, the establishment of a community atmosphere was initiated from the first day of session. Team building workshops and activities were designed to engage students in learning experiences that allowed members to learn to work effectively with all members of the KBC cohort. It was the intention that the students would develop teamwork skills as they acquired problem-solving skills.

In order to enhance the community learning atmosphere the students were housed in a special 'home room'. This room was the physical space in which the students and the four lecturers who facilitated their learning met for all the activities that were at the core of PBL. For the students involved it would appear that friendship and community support have assisted their learning. Because they felt comfortable in their environment they have learnt through participation in face-to-face and via electronic conversation, and KBC class activities. Further they were making use of the communication technology to express opinions.

School-based Learning for Curriculum Development

This source of learning was to provide students with an opportunity to better understand the culture of schools, teaching and classrooms. It was intended that students could achieve this through observing and interviewing teachers, providing support for teachers, and teaching individual and small groups of students. Students were also increasing their awareness that teaching requires skills and practice. Importantly, however, students were gaining an insight and understanding that being a teacher is a commitment and a profession that requires life-long learning. Students needed to be aware of their role in PBL and the preparation phase engaged the students in several workshop and assessment tasks where they worked in small self-directed groups in order to solve open-ended problems. The experience with these tasks helped students realise that PBL required a great deal of honest and open communication in order to establish a common understanding of the coherent social practice needed to successfully complete a task.

The KBC concept supported by computer mediated communication has contributed to the professional socialisation of students by addressing four issues. First, it has helped students to define the profession in which they will work and to realise that they are responsible for the development of the knowledge and skills needed to become a member of the teaching profession. Second, they have developed an understanding of the professional life of teachers and the nature of 'teachers' work'. Third, they have come to realise that there is a body of knowledge that they need to access in order to be educated about the profession, and finally they have developed a sense of professional identity.

The combination of learning from three interacting sources of information of a Knowledge Building Community (KBC): community learning; school-based learning and problem-based learning have enhanced the process of professional socialisation. They have also learnt about the professional life of teachers - the language of the profession, belief systems, symbolic lives. Also by performing a professional role in schools they have developed some sense of professional identity. When students use computer mediated communication in a KBC they can be very creative and forthright in sharing opinions and ideas.

Collaborative Learning

Traditional paper-based distance education approaches are now firmly established within many tertiary education institutions and are widely accepted as a valid form of educational delivery. While many subject areas lend themselves well to distance delivery, there have always been some which did not necessarily adapt well to non face-to-face provision, in particular, those subjects where interpersonal interaction was integral. Online delivery offers new possibilities for teaching and learning in these areas through the added dimension of collaboration and interaction. A new educational literature focused on online teaching and learning is emerging as greater numbers of educational institutions take up the option to deliver their courses in the online environment.

In US, a course for teaching group processes is offered at Southern Cross University and was developed as part of a major initiative by the School of Social and Workplace Development (SaWD) to offer its full undergraduate Bachelor of Social Science (BSocSc) degree online. This degree has majors in such areas as community development, counselling and mediation, human relations and communication, human resource development, politics, social welfare and sociology. The SaWD Online Project, as it became known, is in many respects philosophically and ideologically different from online initiatives at many other institutions in that our definition of 'online development' required full re-design of units, not just 'web mounting' or 'web-enhancing' existing paper-based external materials. It represents more than a technological enhancement of teaching but instead a student-centred, collaborative learning approach as advocated by educators in the constructivist and active learning traditions.

Group Processes is a compulsory unit in the BSocSc degree and has been offered successfully both internally and off-campus. Online teaching approaches provide for collaborative learning in a subject area best taught through interactive experiences. *Group Processes* has been offered successfully for five years both internally (on-campus) and externally (off-campus). For internal students the unit is taught experientially. Activities are designed each week to give students experience in observing group processes within the tutorial; experience in facilitating and leading activities and experience in particular group interactions grounded in established group theories.

All assessments are based on their experiences and learning about group processes in their tutorial groups. External students, on the other hand, have a very different learning experience from those studying internally. They are provided with a book of readings and a study guide, but it is not possible to provide interactive group experiences. Instead students apply theoretical concepts in their workplaces or communities as opportunities to relate theory to practice. Many external students have limited opportunity to experiment with different group processes, such as facilitation, decision making and conflict resolution, a situation that is not entirely satisfactory from our view as adult educators. The SaWD Online project presented a real opportunity to improve the collaborative possibilities for students studying off-campus.

Group Processes was thus selected as one of the early subjects for online development, and was to be trialed with a maximum enrolment of twenty students.While many of the other lecturers developing online materials for the BSocSc designed primarily from their off-campus, print-based course, the developers of *Group Processes* Online gained inspiration for the unit design primarily from the on-campus course, with stronger emphasis on process than content. In keeping with our preference for constructivist, experiential learning, the students' experience of being part of the enrolled group informs their learning and forms the basis of their assessment.

As it was assumed that there would be an enrolment of around twenty students for the initial pilot, we designed a program of activities that was a mixture of small group (maximum of five participants), large group, synchronous (i.e. 'real time') and asynchronous activities, with and without the participation of the tutor. Clear expectations of student participation and tutor involvement were made at the outset. For instance, there was a strong emphasis on peer collaboration and teamwork, made possible by the learning shell used, with a number of activities being student directed. For each of the activities students were allocated a role to assist the group in its process, roles such as discussion leader, facilitator, reporter, observer and participant. Assessment tasks were based on student experiences and included:

- an *observation report*, in which they were to observe interactions in one of the activities and comment on their observations in the light of the theory of Group Processes;
- a *reflective journal*, in which students recorded reflections of their experiences and which aimed to

help them heighten their observational skills, process information, explore their feelings, assess their progress, evaluate their performance, improve communication, and enhance their writing skills and fluency; and

- an *essay* which required students to evaluate the effectiveness of the online group of which they had been a part, drawing on theories of group effectiveness to substantiate their assessment.

The online development of *Group Processes* as an opportunity to observe the extent to which theories about group behaviour which are based on research into face-to-face groups can be applied to group experience in the online environment. In traditional external mode students are very much independent and self-directed and contact the teacher directly when they need assistance. With a face-to-face class, the teacher has a clear role in meeting with the group each week, offering guidance and helping to solve problems. In many ways, the online environment provides an opportunity to build community in ways that are at the same time similar to, but different from, building community in face-to-face settings such as workplaces and neighbourhoods, communities defined by place, rather than by communication.

Groups have a number of characteristics that make them unique and provide a specialised context for communication. These characteristics include interdependence, a common goal, the group's personality, the commitment of group members, and the group's cohesiveness. Other characteristics provide a specialised context: group conflict, social facilitation, gender differences, group size and group norms. All of these aspects were present in this online group experience: interdependence was established from the beginning through the necessity for collaboration to achieve educational goals; the common goal of learning group processes was a clear understanding shared by all participants; the group had a particular sort of personality, grounded very much in the peculiarities of the online environment. Differences were apparent also between communicating synchronously compared with asynchronously. With real time communication, there was more humour and informality, while with delayed communication the students tended to communicate more formally. However, the tutor noticed that when students were communicating synchronously, they gave little attention to their required task or activity, and much more to maintenance actions, such as getting to know each other, sharing jokes, enjoying the novelty of the medium.

When students were required to do particular tasks in asynchronous mode, they were likely to be more formal and less chatty in their communications, but were giving serious thought to course content. This raises the question of the usefulness of synchronous communication educationally. Synchronous communication is also much more subject to the vagaries of technological and service provider capacities. On a number of occasions students were unable to log on at the appointed time, or lost their connection mid conversation. It would seem that learning how to communicate with subtlety and authenticity in this medium will take time - when difficulties arise, it takes longer to clarify and sort out any miscommunication.

While the lack of face-to-face cues can inhibit communication in some ways, some social psychologists have argued that more intense relationships can be built with the removal of face-to-face inhibitions. An interesting development was the way the group perceived the role of the teacher. In the online environment, where there are only words on a screen, different skills and teaching strategies are called for. Researchers into group behaviour suggest that groups, whatever their purpose, have a life cycle, often progressing through recognisable developmental stages. The most familiar model is that described by Tuckman: forming; storming; norming; performing and mourning. It would seem that any group is likely to have a developmental experience, and the online group was no exception. Experienced educators and researchers in online education indicate that online groups do have a similar life cycle.

Students initially felt that the group did not go through a storming period, as there appeared to be no conflict between members. However, the enormous technological difficulties and frustrations that led to many having to leave the course created great anxiety among the remaining members of the group which prevented the group from moving into the norming and performing stages. It was not until the course was reorganised and put back on track in the light of the disruptions that the group could then relax into its task of completing the required activities as a whole group of five.

The main problems encountered in teaching *Group Processes* online were technological in nature and origin: lack of student preparation and understanding of the particular course shell used; differential online familiarity and technological skill; and significant attrition rates due partly to frustrations with negotiating the technology. These problems were exacerbated by an over-ambitious course design which incorporated significant levels of interdependence, necessitating frequent reorganisation and consolidation of groups. A more cautious attitude towards what is feasible within technological constraints and greater understanding of the communication issues likely to be encountered in online collaboration would reduce the likelihood of the kind of frustrations we experienced. Furthermore, we would argue that taking on online delivery significantly increases the amount of time taken in distance delivery and should be reflected appropriately in teaching load allocations. While much of our experience reveals a cautionary tale, there is no doubt that significant learning about group processes occurred and the students who remained in the course developed a sophisticated understanding of the interactive potentials and issues faced in online collaboration. The flexibility offered by the online environment allowed opportunities for course redesign to meet the needs of the particular group, flexibility that is not possible in traditional distance education.

Fulfilling the Needs of Networked Communities

Cultural norms of individualism, structural conditions in schools, teachers' differing pedagogical orientations, as well as the absence of common beliefs and expectations or "shared professional identity" all stifle teachers' abilities to collaborate. Organizational structures of schooling, "how school space is arranged; how content and students are organized in grade levels; how time is allotted to tasks; and how organizational rules govern the behavior and performance of both adults and students," have meant that instructional practices over the last century have remained consistently teacher-centered despite various reform efforts. Open classroom reforms in the 1970's did little to alter the seclusion and independence of classroom instruction. As such, teachers have traditionally had limited impetus to share and collaborate over instruction. Distributed teachers have had even less opportunity to collaborate.

The Learning in Networked Communities (LiNC) project encourages distributed teacher collaboration by developing and deploying innovative collaborative technology in science classrooms. A major outcome of this project is the collaborative software called The Virtual School. While the LiNC project began as a study of collaborative software use by students, it generated a great deal of understanding of and attention to new problems associated with teacher collaborations. The student collaborations facilitated by LiNC obligated *teachers* to collaborate; however, teacher collaboration has never been a well-established or well-supported practice. In designing and implementing networked-based student collaborative activities, LiNC teachers themselves faced new kinds of collaborative challenges and opportunities. In these novel collaborative arrangements, teachers confronted unique problems relating to awareness and assessment of student activities, communication among teachers, scheduling and planning for different subjects and schools, as well as pedagogical and stylistic differences.

A significant portion of the LiNC project was devoted to the development and evaluation of the Virtual School. This software is a continually evolving Java-based network application designed to allow students to collaborate across classroom boundaries. Students used a variety of communication and collaborative tools integrated into the Virtual School to work and learn in cooperative groups across grade level, subject, and school. The client side of the Virtual School application consists of a main control window that integrates email, chat, video-conferencing, application sharing, whiteboard, and collaborative writing tools. Teachers located in different classrooms in different schools experience very different environments seen in students, local culture, school administration, and setting.

Computer technology allows new forms of collaboration over time and place, bridging differences and breaking down spatial and temporal barriers.

Electronic collaboration tools "allow learners control of time and place when and where learning transpires". This control by students forced teachers to reconsider how they monitor, interact, control, and assess student work. Use of the Virtual School forced LiNC teachers to collaborate with each other and to do so in new ways. In order to coordinate the use of the rich modes of collaboration offered by the Virtual School, teachers created parallel curriculum across school, age, and ability with integrated tasks, schedules, grading, deadlines, and benchmarks. Teachers coordinated synchronous and asynchronous interactions of distributed groups.

Teaching in public school has always been somewhat chaotic. Slight adjustments on one level can cause major disruptions on another level. Coordinating schedules across schools compounds many of these problems. As a result, teachers encounter significantly new and greater challenges when collaborating with one another. Computer-mediated activities bring new abilities and problems to teachers' routine work; and therefore, tools like the Virtual School that connect distant classrooms can demand radical shifts in instructional practices. Collaboration required a great deal of face-to-face work, much more than teachers expected. Despite significant planning, teachers in LiNC confronted several organizational challenges resulting from their need to coordinate Virtual School activities. These included conflicts and shifts in school scheduling, administration, network and computer resources, planning, and assessment. Even schools in the same system can operate on different schedules, and for small school systems, coordinating science class schedules across schools requires a great deal of additional effort and planning. Despite cooperative administration and extensive pre-planning, teachers may be unable to precisely align schedules.

In order to take advantage of the synchronous capabilities of the technology, teachers needed to synchronize their work. Major difficulties arose when a teacher was unable to be assigned the class schedule she needed to conduct synchronous collaborative activities. School system administration is also complex and distributed. There are few central information systems that give personnel the ability to realize and control the implications and effects of administrative decisions.

Commitment from school administrators early in the project assured researchers that teachers and classrooms participating in the collaborations would have a common time slot. Over a five-year period, this goal was never fully achieved. Teachers had little control over or knowledge of scheduling prior to it being announced as a final mandate. Administrations routinely kept schedules "secret" prior to their announcement to meet conflicting demands. As a result, teachers were forced to use planning periods, pull students from other classes, and complete collaborative project work after school. In many cases, this was testimony to the resourcefulness of teachers, that is, their ability to negotiate and improvise in the face of less than ideal circumstances.

Network technology adds new opportunities, but it also adds a new dimension to this organizational chaos. For example, a seemingly benign decision was made by school administrators to route the school system's Ethernet connections through a firewall for practical reasons other than security and filtering. This caused problems for a variety of LiNC *and* non-LiNC teacher and student activities. For instance, the firewall eliminated the ability to videoconference outside of the school systems network. Unfortunately, this came at a time when the teachers were gearing up for a second year of a large project involving community mentors that would benefit greatly from the ability to videoconference. Teachers were strongly encouraged into collaborating and at the same time confined to their closed classrooms and routines. Although they were each allotted a planning period, their schedules allowed no mutual time to plan and coordinate activities with teachers at other schools. Teachers met after school on their own time.

Ironically, teachers felt the need to meet face-to-face to coordinate efforts effectively rather than meet remotely using the Virtual School. In order to meet face-to-face, LiNC teachers had to drive across the county. While they met more frequently as the project progressed, it was still not enough to allow sufficient communication. Circumstances were extremely dynamic. Without the ability to talk daily, informally in hallways and immediately following class, major breakdowns in communication were inevitable. One striking example of organizational chaos ensuing from teachers' lack of ability to communicate frequently about the project activities centered on the use of deadlines or due dates for student groups by teachers. A shift in emphasis from short-term to long-term projects resulted in a greater need for common deadlines mainly because of the degree to which work became distributed among students and sub-groups. Subsequent shifts in deadlines became a major source of problems.

The Virtual School afforded teachers the ability to easily connect synchronous and asynchronous work of remote groups. Remote groups in many cases produced a group-authored product in the end, but in doing so, students and teachers needed to coordinate deadlines in order to avoid missing or unfinished pieces of the groups' work. Teachers wrestled with how to establish deadlines in Virtual School projects given conflicting local versus distributed constraints. When synchronous and asynchronous group work is linked as with much Virtual School work, small changes in deadlines can cause serious planning difficulties. Encouraging inter-reliance through the collaborative features of the technology increased the chance of deeper collaborations, but it also increased the chaos of organizing the group work by extending and distributing the network of inter-relations among classrooms.

A number of issues related to teachers' awareness of student activities across remote collaborative groups arise as a direct result of the physical and temporal dispersion of events and causes triggered by Virtual School activities. Tracking student groups locally in the classroom is difficult; spreading out groups among different classrooms and periods via computer-mediated communications, and directing student attention toward computer-mediated group work further detaches teachers from usual channels of awareness of group activity.

When student interaction is directed at a computer screen rather than the teacher or co-present peer, teachers have limited view of the interaction. As a result, remote teachers may have very different perceptions of the same computer-mediated interaction. For example in one long-term project, students were having difficulty collaborating. The evaluation data clearly showed the groups were struggling with their interactions. The frequency of chat and email decreased significantly as the activity progressed to the point where little or no attempt to communicate was initiated by either side. Some communications were blatantly hostile, and planning was intentionally non-collaborative in that they made decisions to work on independent products unlike other groups.

Teachers were forced to more actively monitor group work and to provide more individual attention to an overwhelming classroom, but unless they asked the right people the right questions at the right time, misleading perceptions were inevitable. Lack of experience and context limited teachers' ability to know the right kinds of questions to ask. Students experienced awareness problems themselves because they lacked an understanding of the remote teachers' expectations and requirements for the group. In facing these awareness problems, teachers were often forced to reflect on their own habits, practices, and "technical culture".

Traditionally, teachers have been accustomed to and reliant on individualistic norms and practices. This suggests that greater autonomy in teaching means less opportunity for collaboration; however, autonomy in teaching practices does not necessarily oppose collaborative goals. In fact, some argue that people can become *more* autonomous through working effectively and cooperatively with others. The use of collaborative computing confronted teachers in LiNC with a number of particular problems concerning grading, planning, and coordinating collaborative activities of students. Teachers were coupled with other teachers by the collaborations of their students, and their normal individualistic teaching practices often conflicted due to the nature and level of the teacher collaboration demanded of them.

In traditional collaborative arrangements, teachers are often co-located in the same classroom or school. As such, they have direct access to a wide variety of common cues and conditions that inform their practices. Computers allow teachers in diverse settings to collaborate, but compared to face-to-face interaction, they also obscure and disconnect teachers from one another. LiNC teachers changed deadlines, requirements, and procedures without notifying each other. Teachers prepared students differently. They disagreed on the degree of student autonomy in planning, and they varied in the degree of intervention and types of help provided to the collaborative groups. Despite agreement on a common grading rubric, teachers reverted to individual ways of assessing group projects.

While computers joined their work, teachers did not have the luxury of interacting in person on a daily basis as with same school collaborations to which they have been accustomed. "Isolated settings compel teachers in opposite direction—toward norms of self-reliance. Under these circumstances, requests and offers of assistance seem far less apt to occur". LiNC teachers recognized their isolation as teachers and, to some degree, hoped that the technology could alleviate some of it. However, with the enhanced levels of contact and interaction at a distance provided by the collaborative technology came greater opportunities to clash over individuality and idiosyncrasies. Two key examples of such clashes in the LiNC project arose as a result of the tightly knit but distant collaborations engendered by the use of the technology. Because of the physical disconnection of teachers' work and the demands of joining students with computers, differences in teachers' styles and assessment goals became extremely important.

Although LiNC teachers shared a great deal of general pedagogical beliefs and attitudes, they varied significantly in how they enacted the curriculum in their particular classrooms. All LiNC teachers valued hands-on and student-guided projects, and they all valued the curricular and "real-world" technical skills encouraged by the projects.

Although collaborative computing offers new opportunities, "teachers cannot be expected to reorganize classrooms to provide this type of experience for students while they themselves remain in the isolation of the traditional classroom". Two key features of computer-supported collaboration exacerbated the already chaotic organizational problems of teachers.

1) Collaborations among distant teachers promoted contention related to clashes of individuality and style, and

2) on-line technologies disperse events and their causes in space and time.

Teachers need to derive information from, monitor the use of, and utilize the special resources that computer network technology makes available. Moreover, planning for remote collaborative work needs to be more flexible and relaxed to allow for instructional differences. To combat the additional organizational chaos and conflict engendered by collaborative technology, teachers need ways to stabilize and filter information about computer-mediated collaborations. They need quick and easy access to the information that is most salient to their planning. They need notification of salient information and feedback about student progress and problems as well as teaching changes, and they need ways of managing computer group work that allow for a better understanding of the actions of computer-mediated groups and their instructors and a better ability for teachers to make adjustments.

Telecollaborative Activities

Bridging the gap between theory and practice has been a challenge for teacher education programs for many decades.

John Dewey encouraged teacher education programs to prepare teachers to reflect upon theoretical issues and their relationship to practical classroom application. Nearly twenty years later, Zeichner called for development of reflective teachers who critically analyze classroom situations. Case-based learning originated in business and law schools and has recently been used in teacher education in an attempt to bridge the gap between theory and practice. Benefits of applying cases to teacher education include

- development of critical analysis and problem solving skills,
- opportunities for reflective practice,
- analysis and decision-making in complex situations,
- active learning, and
- creation of a community of learners.

In the 21st century, technological advances have made it possible to improve traditional case-based learning with multimedia features that enhance authenticity and active learning. For example, technology allows us to go beyond the traditional one-dimensional text-based case study to include features such as audio and video clips. Technological advances have also made it possible to extend the learning community beyond the walls of traditional teacher education courses. Preservice teacher education learning communities are being redefined to include participants from geographically disparate locations, experienced classroom teachers, and university instructors.

As technical capabilities continue to improve, cross-university collaborations receive increased attention. This is particularly true in the teacher education community. Collaboration among teacher education programs allows students to "share ideas and opinions, jointly develop materials, and gain new perspectives." It also enables students to make scholarly and personal connections that may support them during their induction years. Social studies teacher education programs have a responsibility to "build ongoing and stimulating collaborative links among social studies educators". Likewise, teacher education programs have a responsibility to prepare prospective teachers to know and apply educational theory so that professional knowledge is considered when making classroom decisions.

Newsgroups, which utilize Networked News Transport Protocol (NNTP), were selected over other popular asynchronous communication methods such as electronic mail and listservs (Simple Mail Transport Protocol), web-based discussion groups (Hypertext Transport Protocol) for several reasons. The reasons include the ability to organize dialogue around a specific theme or thread, the ability to keep track of the read and unread messages, accessibility from both Microsoft Internet Explorer and Netscape Communicator, avoidance of excessive messages delivered to personal email accounts, and the ability to mirror the newsgroup with remote sites which alleviates excessive connection delays. Newsgroup administrators from the University of Virginia and the University of Florida arranged to exchange the newsgroup between the two universities.

Students most frequently discussed knowledge related to generic teaching issues. Discussions of content-specific knowledge were primarily related to searching for and sharing new teaching ideas and strategies. Students discussed a wide range of generic teaching issues throughout this project. Most of these issues were intentionally embedded within the case and included issues related to grouping students, communicating with parents, assessment, organization skills such as note taking, communicating objectives with students, selecting age appropriate content, student motivation, mentoring, school culture and community, noise level in the classroom, technology integration issues, and planning.

Since the students were primarily novice teachers, generic issues such as classroom management, planning, and student grouping were probably at the forefront of their thoughts. Many students integrated their professional knowledge and experience with Julia's experiences to reflect upon their beliefs about teaching and learning, lessons they had learned in the past, and their decision to become a teacher. Students also reflected on their participation in the telecollaborative activity. It is essential that teacher education programs provide students opportunities for reflection so that they will enter the field as reflective practitioners. Zeichner promoted this paradigm of teacher education, arguing, "the fundamental task of teacher education from this point is to develop prospective teachers' capacities for reflective action and to help examine the moral, ethical and political issues, as well as the instrumental issues, that are embedded in their everyday thinking and practice".

By expanding the traditional preservice cohort group to include both inservice teachers and geographically remote peers, students were empowered to participate in authentic professional dialogue. While the inclusion of inservice teachers was restricted to those enrolled in one of the participating courses, their influence on the preservice teachers was evident. Students reported that they particularly enjoyed reading the responses from the inservice teachers and that they found the responses extremely valuable. Likewise, most of the inservice teachers valued their participation and reported that the postings from preservice teachers helped them be more supportive of new teachers in their own building. Inservice teachers also reported that they appreciated the opportunity to candidly discuss their feelings via the newsgroups because they often feel they must converse cautiously because of the schoolwide "rumor mill." These inservice teachers just happened to be enrolled in the courses and while three of the four reported enjoying the experience one was extremely negative about his participation and reported that he "got sick of" having to communicate with teachers in training.

Interaction within this telecollaborative project was less than ideal. Students more frequently communicated with their local peers than with their geographically disparate peers. This counters many of the goals of cross-university collaboration such as sharing ideas and gaining multiple perspectives. While students reported benefiting from exchanges with both local and geographically disparate peers, we were not satisfied with the interaction that occurred during the project or with the types of interaction, that occurred. This is not a unique phenomenon, and some claim individuals need to be engaged in a controversial topic to spark dynamic interactions.

9

Skills Development for Modern Teaching

The teacher plays a key role in determining not only how but how well technologies are used in classrooms, and thus the extent to which technologies improve student performance. Given the central importance of teachers in the application of technologies for teaching and learning, education policy makers must quickly turn their attention to teachers: their readiness and how best to prepare them to use the technology infrastructure policy makers have been working so hard to create. Competent teachers apply broad, deep, and integrated sets of knowledge and skills as they plan for, implement, and revise instruction. Technology proficiency is but one dimension of teacher competence.

A review of research on teacher knowledge and teaching standards suggests that over time effective teachers develop the following skills and behaviors:

- Teachers know how to plan, prepare for, and design effective curriculum, assessment tools, and instruction strategies.
- Teachers are skilled instructional facilitators.
- Teachers are reflective practitioners.

- Teachers are professionals committed to lifelong learning.
- Teachers know how to direct students through course content.
- Teachers know how to assess and evaluate student work, how to provide effective feedback, and how to apply what they have learned to improve instruction.
- Teachers know and can utilize effectively a repertoire of instructional and communication strategies.
- Teachers are effective classroom managers and know how to motivate students.
- Teachers understand how children learn and develop.
- Teachers know the subject matter they teach.
- Teachers are adept at locating, creating, and using curriculum resources and technologies.
- Teachers embrace student diversity, understand the community context, and know how to identify the strengths and needs of individual students.

Acquisition of technology knowledge and skills must be concomitant with the development of a broader array of competencies. Technology is perceived as a means to an end rather than as an end in itself. Early attempts to develop technology standards for teachers were isolated from the broader teacher competencies and were focused primarily on technology skills. Consequently these competencies were largely ignored by teacher-training institutions. Typically, colleges of education simply required a single media course to satisfy accreditation requirements; often, colleges were reluctant to insert yet another course into an already overloaded curriculum. The International Society for Technology in Education

(ISTE) has actively addressed the technology isolation problem and has recently released a set of revised teacher technology standards.

Developed through a rigorous process of expert and lay-person input, the NETS-T Project (National Educational Technology Standards for Teachers) explicitly describes what competent teachers should know and should be able to do with technology in the context of broader teacher competencies. The NETS-T standards are categorized as follows:

– technology operations and concepts,
– planning and designing learning environments and experiences,
– teaching, learning, and the curriculum,
– assessment and evaluation,
– productivity and professional practice,
– social, ethical, legal, and human issues.

None of these categories, with the exception of technology operations and concepts, contains the term "technology." Moreover, it is easy to align these six categories with the broader teacher competencies presented above. These facts support the generally accepted view that technology should be used as an enabling strategy that supports and extends the various functions of teaching and learning. This approach is also more palatable to curriculum reformers in that it is more relevant to and aligned with the larger work of education-systems reform. Because of this integrated approach, the revised ISTE standards are now taken seriously. The U.S. Department of Education's PT3 initiative (Preparing Tomorrow's Teachers to Use

Technology), for example, is driving a major effort by universities and colleges nationwide to reorganize their teacherpreparation curricula, field experiences, induction programs, and collaboration with arts and sciences departments.

The NETS-T standards, especially when aligned with the Interstate New Teacher Assessment and Support Consortium (INTASC) standards, is at the heart of this higher-education reform movement and is generating heightened awareness of the importance and content of teacher standards in general and technology-integration competencies in particular. Further, the new NETS-T standards are explicitly aligned with the NETS for students. These standards specify what students should know and be able to do with technology as a result of their school's curriculum. To emphasize technology integration, ISTE developed a collection of profiles and scenarios that illustrate what classrooms look like when technology is integrated effectively and what technology standards students attain as a result. To live, learn, and work successfully in an increasingly complex and information-rich society, students must be able to use technology effectively. Within an effective educational setting, technology can enable students to become:

- Capable information technology users
- Information seekers, analyzers, and evaluators
- Problem solvers and decision makers
- Creative and effective users of productivity tools
- Communicators, collaborators, publishers, and producers
- Informed, responsible, and contributing citizens

In fact, the teacher standards are purposefully intended to help teachers develop strategies that will enable their students to attain the student-technology standards as well as the content standards.

Called the "NETS for Students" project, these standards are:

1. Basic operations and concepts:
   - Students demonstrate a sound understanding of the nature and operation of technology systems.
   - Students are proficient in the use of technology.
2. Social, ethical, and human issues:
   - Students understand the ethical, cultural, and societal issues related to technology.
   - Students practice responsible use of technology systems, information, and software.
   - Students develop positive attitudes toward technology uses that support lifelong learning, collaboration and productivity.
3. Technology productivity tools:
   - Students use technology tools to enhance learning, increase productivity, and promote creativity.
   - Students use productivity tools to collaborate in constructing technology-enhanced models, prepare publications, and produce other creative works.
4. Technology communications tools:
   - Students use telecommunications to collaborate, publish, and interact with peers, experts, and other audiences.

- Students use a variety of media and formats to communicate information and ideas effectively to multiple audiences.

5. Technology research tools:

   - Students use technology to locate, evaluate, and collect information from a variety of sources.
   - Students use technology tools to process data and report results.
   - Students evaluate and select new information resources and technological innovations on the basis of appropriateness for specific tasks.

6. Technology problem-solving and decision-making tools:

   - Students use technology resources for solving problems and making informed decisions.
   - Students employ technology in the development of strategies for solving problems in the real world.

Research over the past decade has also supplied evidence that teachers go through predictable stages of development as they develop technology-integration competence. The Apple Classrooms of Tomorrow research described these stages as:

- entry
- adoption
- adaptation
- appropriation
- transformation.

Developing Teaching Skills

Given the importance of well-trained teachers for technologies to be effective in enhancing learning, what might education policy makers do to support and encourage appropriate strategies for training teachers? No single approach to professional development will meet the learning needs of all teachers seeking to develop skills and knowledge in the integration and application of technology.

Teachers progress through a series of five predictable stages as their expertise in technology adoption and integration evolves. It is likely that within a school, and certainly within a district, teachers will exhibit varying levels of expertise and therefore a variety of different professional-development opportunities will be required. To the extent possible, it is desirable to provide a continuum of professional-development opportunities so that the learning needs of teachers at all stages in the continuum will be met. This is easy to say, but hard to do with the limited time and money available for training. Professional development is increasingly designed with intent to establish collegiality, encourage experimentation and risk-taking, and promote discourse, reflection, and collaboration. There are a number of commonly held beliefs about the characteristics of effective professional development.

- The ultimate goal of high-quality professional development is to improve student learning.
- Professional development should focus upon enhancing student academic achievement. The development of teacher proficiency in the integration and application of technology must be linked to

student learning of the subject matter and satisfaction of state and local content standards.

- Professional development is most effective when the learner has an opportunity to participate in decision-making that concerns its design and delivery. Often, even in a content or skill area that is new to her, a teacher is in the best position to determine what his or her learning needs are and how best to engage in that learning. This recommendation is consistent with the adult-education literature. Adults possess a self-concept characterized by a need to be self-directed. Therefore, adult learners, including teachers, often resent and resist those situations, including professional-development activities, where they believe that others are imposing their beliefs—or their training—upon them.

- Professional-development activities associated with technology often produce anxiety in teachers who recognize and worry about the disparity in skills and knowledge between themselves and their colleagues. When teachers are involved in the development of training programs, it diminishes their anxiety and ensures that their own personal learning needs will be met.

- High-quality professional development is rigorous and sustained over time. Historically, professional-development offerings have been delivered in a "one-in-a-row" format that prevents any cumulative or significant learning outcome. The mastery of technology integration requires repeated cycles of professional development that keep pace with advances in technology and research.

- Teachers need time to reflect upon what they have learned, to integrate new knowledge into practice through experimentation, to reflect upon the outcomes of changes made in their practice, and to make further adjustments as needed. An effective professional-development program, according to Corcoran, provides "sufficient time and follow-up support for teachers to master new content and strategies and to integrate them into practice."
- Professional development is most effective when it addresses authentic problems that teachers face when integrating technology into their classrooms and when technology is linked with broader reform goals of school or district improvement. Adults are motivated to engage in learning to the extent that they perceive the activity enabling them to better perform tasks or manage problems. Adults acquire new knowledge, skills, and attitudes most effectively when they are able to learn within a context that is congruent with that of their own practice. Consequently, professional development for teachers is most effective when it is relevant to their subject matter and/or grade level. This also means that while engaging in a professional-development activity, teachers should utilize the same technology that they will be using when they teach their students.
- Professional development that is designed to elevate teacher proficiency in the integration and application of technology is most effective when it is not conducted as an isolated initiative. Minimally, professional development aimed to elevate teacher technology competencies should be offered as an integral component of the school technology plan; optimally, it should be offered as an integral component of school

or district reform initiatives to facilitate improved student academic achievement.

- High-quality professional development contributes to the establishment of a collegial and collaborative culture. Effective professional development is characterized by the development of learning communities where staff work toward commonly held goals, colleagues exchange ideas and knowledge and provide constructive feedback and encouragement to their peers, and innovation and accomplishment are publicly acknowledged.
- Effective professional development incorporates evaluation to ensure that each activity is meeting the learning needs of its participants. There are three types of evaluation that should be built into every professional-development program: performative evaluation, formative evaluation, and summative evaluation. A variety of methods of data collection should be employed and multiple sources of information should be consulted. Collectively, these three forms of evaluation contribute to the ongoing assessment of a professional-development program, providing data to inform adjustments that ensure that the program is meeting its objectives.

A comprehensive approach to providing professional development includes both formal and informal opportunities for teachers. Formal approaches to professional development encompass those activities that occur largely under the direction of an educator or trainer who assumes the role of mediating the learning. Under these circumstances, the instructor is likely to be responsible for identifying learning objectives, determining appropriate formats and instructional techniques, and establishing evaluation crite Formal Thrning typically involves some sort of organizational or ritiesmunity sponsorship.

f child n contrast, learning that occurs outside the confines devel ograms provided by institutions is considered nce, mal learning. Informal learning, sometimes referred d sos self-directed learning, typically occurs in the learner's "natural setting" and is initiated and conducted independently. The learner determines his or her own objectives, the manner in which learning will take place, and the appropriate resources. Self-directed learning does not necessarily mean learning alone. Adults often interact with other people and even groups of people in their selfdirected learning pursuits. Policy makers may want to consider both kinds of approaches.

Formal Approaches

Conferences, Institutes, and Workshops

There are occasions when well-designed workshops or conferences are an appropriate method of professional development. These activities are useful methods for introducing specific skills to a learner audience, such as how to use a particular software application or how to navigate the Internet, particularly when follow-up support will be provided. Thoughtfully designed conferences and workshops are structured so that they provide opportunities for participants to interact and collaborate, learning together and from each other. They can also provide a venue for learners to meet their electronic mentors, colleagues, and/or instructors in a face-toface setting, thus sustaining professional development that is conducted at a distance.

Courses and Classes

Enrollment in a program of study provided by an institution of higher education is another traditional approach to professional development. Teachers may enroll in classes to advance their professional growth and at the same time accumulate graduate credit that facilitates salary-schedule movement.

Action Research and Study Groups

Action research is an approach to professional development in which teachers typically spend one or more years engaged in classroom-based research projects. Loucks-Horsley et al. describe action research as a process in which teachers examine their practice and associated student learning, engage in meaningful conversations about their reflections with their colleagues, and share their findings in descriptive written reports. As a professional-development activity, action research can be tailored to the level of expertise and the learning needs of individual teachers. When action research is conducted collaboratively, it fosters the growth of a learning community.

Distance Learning

Technology plays a significant role in transcending some of the constraints associated with traditional modes of formal professional development. Distance learning allows an instructor and students to interact with one another, independent of space and time, by utilizing interactive computer conferencing, video and/or audio tape, conventional reading materials, radio, the Internet, or any combination thereof. Professional development delivered at a distance enables teachers to enroll for credit courses at universities located around the world. Although many of these programs continue to follow traditional university format where learning is instructor-centered, new models of instruction are emerging. Technology changes the way that people teach and learn, not only in K-12 classrooms but in virtual higher-education classrooms as well. Distance learning offers the advantages of flexibility in time and location and provides teachers with a vast array of resources. Furthermore, participation in professional development that is electronically delivered enables teachers to interact with peers that bring with them a rich diversity in culture, perspective, and experience.

Informal Approaches

Professional development that is embedded in the practice of teaching. "Informal and job-embedded processes are essential to support and extend learning that takes place in workshops and in classes". Teachers learn from their daily practice.

Observation

Observation is an example of an informal and job-embedded approach to professional development. Observation is a process that is mutually beneficial to the person being observed and the observer. The individual being observed learns from the feedback provided about instructional practice and classroom management; the observer also learns from this process by viewing and reflecting upon the strategies and techniques employed by a colleague. Communication between the teacher being observed and the observer contributes further to the professional-development activity. The disadvantages of utilizing this approach to professional development include the need to hire a substitute to cover the time spent out of the classroom engaged in observation. In order for this exercise to be truly beneficial, the observer needs to be somewhat conversant in the strategy or technique being modeled so that accurate and constructive feedback may be rendered. It is also important that the observer is cognizant of appropriate methods for providing feedback that is constructive and encouraging rather than disparaging.

Mentoring

Mentoring involves pairing teachers who are skilled in a particular instructional technique or strategy with one or more novice teachers. In order for mentoring to be an effective professional-development activity, careful matching of partners is required instead of haphazard pairing. And, of course, the person doing the mentoring must have knowledge and skills that can be passed on. In order to be effective, a mentor must have the necessary time to devote to the mentoring relationship. Mentors can provide advice, reassurance, encouragement, and technical assistance (NFIE). Because of their expertise, mentors are able to serve as role models and to provide objective feedback. To benefit from this approach to professional development, mentees must be willing to accept assistance.

Mentors also experience professional growth by engaging in reflection upon the questions asked by their mentees and upon the knowledge that they bring to the task, by formulating a response that is relevant to the context, and by exercising leadership. Recognition, compensation, and professional development in the area of mentoring provide incentives for individuals to accept mentoring roles. Mentoring can take place at a common site or at a distance utilizing technology. Long-distance mentoring can be accomplished using e-mail, written correspondence, and telephone conversations. However, occasional face-to-face meetings are critical to the success of a mentoring relationship.

Teacher Networks and Online Communities

Teachers can also join professional networks to communicate about important issues, to gain troubleshooting assistance, to obtain alternative perspectives for problem solving, to share reflections, and to trade resources. Local networks and electronic networks both have the potential to break the barriers of teacher isolation and to establish a community of practice. The virtual nature of electronic networks can eliminate barriers of position and status that might otherwise be inhibiting in face-to-face interactions (NFIE). They also provide the opportunity for teachers to model online networking for their students.

As an effective approach to professional development, online networks are characterized by regular communication, collaborative problem solving, and skilled facilitation. The literature suggests that the creation of temporary strands around topics of interest is the most effective way to organize electronic forums (NFIE). Increases in bandwidth and advancements in the development of networking software suggest that the use of online communities will continue to evolve as an approach to professional development in the Pacific region.

These are some of the strategies a district or entity might consider in preparing its teachers to use technologies. Some of these strategies might be appropriate in some districts, while others are just not feasible. These are matters policy makers must decide. But regardless of which strategy is selected, there are some general characteristics of effective professional development.

Technology Infrastructure and Policy Issues

For education policy makers, the need for trained teachers to capitalize on investments in technology infrastructure is obvious but not so easily accomplished. The policy issues to be considered include the following:

- What policies will encourage teachers to acquire the necessary knowledge and skills in the use of technologies?
- What policies will sustain support for teachers to use technologies?
- How will teacher use of technologies be evaluated?

For many teachers, having access to technologies is not viewed initially as a benefit. Teachers may consider technologies yet another demand on their time, a set of tools they did not ask for and do not know how to use. Some teachers feel they are already doing a good job in the classroom and wonder how technologies will contribute to improvements. Still other teachers, of course, welcome the technologies and are eager to learn how to use them. In general, policy makers may wish to consider a variety of ways to motivate and support teachers to gain technology competencies. One way is to mandate that all teachers gain these competencies. This mandate might be accomplished in several ways, including making the acquisition of needed knowledge and skills a part of teacher certification, or a prerequisite to pay increases. It might be possible to require new teachers to demonstrate technology competencies before they are hired. Policies that mandate activities such as acquiring or demonstrating technology skills do work in some circumstances. In the Pacific, a number of entities are reviewing their current licensing and credentialing policies, so it may be a good time to add requirements pertaining to technologies. On the other hand, it may prove to be a challenge to mandate technology skills if new or continuing teachers have no convenient way to gain those skills.

Policy makers may wish to consider establishing policy that makes it convenient and feasible for a teacher to learn about technologies by creating conditions under which professional development for teachers is more available. This will most often become a financial issue as professional development costs money. There are several possible ways such policy might be enacted. For example, an entity may set policy that a minimum number of professional-development days be established, some of which are to focus on technology applications. Or teachers might need to be paid to take online courses pertaining to technology applications.

An entity may wish to employ a person or persons with technology training and experience to tutor teachers in technology use. Policies that either mandate or provide opportunities will cost money, but without the establishment of policy that mandates or provides professional-development opportunities, teachers are unlikely to acquire the skills they need to use the technologies available to them, thus negating the potential benefits of the investment that has been made in infrastructure. It is very important for teachers to acquire knowledge and skills in how to use technologies.

But once teachers begin to acquire such skills and begin to use technologies, there is a need to provide means of continuing support to teacher use of technologies. That is, initial training of teachers is not likely to guarantee that the technology infrastructure will continue to be used.

The issue for education policy makers concerns the extent to which a teacher uses technologies effectively can or should be an important criterion in evaluating a teacher's performance. This is a complicated issue for policy makers. On the one hand, to encourage use of technologies, it may be necessary to create policy that recognizes quality performance using technologies, and at the same time reflects negatively on those who do not use technologies. On the other hand, it must be recognized that good teaching is not necessarily dependent on technology utilization. The education system does not want to penalize highly effective teachers who do not use technologies.

Bibliography

Acheson, Keith A.; Gall, Meredith, *Techniques in the Clinical Supervision of Teachers: Preservice and Inservice Applications,* New York: Longman, 1980.

Andrews, Helen Katherine Mary, "A Study of Associate Teachers' Conference Practices With Student Teachers", *Thesis,* University of Toronto, 1980.

Ansara, Joseph, "A Comparison in Practice Teaching Patterns Between Faculty of Education, University of Toronto and Toronto Teachers' *College Student Teachers in the Junior High School, Thesis,* University of Toronto, 1973.

Beegle, Charles W.; Brandt, Richard M., eds, *Observational Methods in the classroom,* Washington, D.C.: Association for Supervision and Curriculum Development, 1973.

Beyer, Landon E. and others, *Preparing Teachers as Professionals,* New York: Teachers College Press, 1989.

Bramwell, John R.; Bramwell, Lillian, "Opinions of First Year Teachers Regarding Their Educational Preparation and Their Present Teaching Experience", *A report for the Teacher Education Committee of the Ontario Public School Mean Teachers' Federation,* 1976.

Broderick, Maria, editor, *For Teachers about Teaching,* Cambridge: Harvard Educational Review, 1988.

Bullough, Robert V., *First-Year Teacher: a Case Study,* New York: Teachers College Press, 1989.

Burke, Peter, *Teacher Development: Induction, Renewal, and Redirection*, New York: Falmer Press, 1987.

Newton, Anne, *Mentoring: a Resource and Training Guide for Educators*, Andover, MA: The Regional Laboratory, 1994.

Noffke, Susan E.; Stevenson, Robert B., editors, *Educational Action Research: Becoming Practically Critical*, New York: Teachers College Press, 1995.

Pearson, Allen T., *The Teacher: Theory and Practice in Teacher Education*, New York: Routledge, 1989.

Peruniak, W.S.; Wahlstrom, M.W.; Weinstein, E.L., *Selection of Applicants to a Faculty of Education: A Case Study*, Toronto: Commission on Declining School Enrolments in Ontario, 1978.

Peters, R.S., *Education and the Education of Teachers*, London, Routledge & Kegan Paul, 1977.

Index